Twayne's English Authors Series

Sylvia E. Bowman, *Editor*

INDIANA UNIVERSITY

William Harrison Ainsworth

TEAS 138

WILLIAM HARRISON AINSWORTH

By GEORGE J. WORTH

University of Kansas

Twayne Publishers, Inc. : : New York

PR
4003
.W6

66958

PREFACE

This is the first full-length study of the novels of William Harrison Ainsworth to be published. To examine his copious output as a novelist in chronological order would result in a shapeless, repetitious, and probably quite unreadable book. I have chosen, therefore, to start with a general chapter giving the relevant details of his long life and career and placing him in the literary milieu of his age, and then, in each of five succeeding chapters, to consider the major aspects of his art.

I have not dealt, except incidentally, with Ainsworth's work as a writer of poems, short stories, and plays, or as an editor. For the most part, this portion of his work—though rather considerable in volume—is scattered, difficult to locate and identify, and, more importantly, of little significance to literary history or criticism. In a short book I have taken it as a task of sufficient magnitude to come to terms with Ainsworth's forty-one novels; it is surely among these that Ainsworth's claim to notice by twentieth-century readers must be found. An Appendix summarizes—rather baldly, it may appear—the plots of Ainsworth's novels, except for those summarized earlier in the book; despite their obvious shortcomings, these synopses will, I hope, serve some useful function.

There has been some disagreement among earlier writers about Ainsworth concerning the canon of his work as a novelist. I am convinced that *Sir John Chiverton*, which is often regarded as a collaborative effort with John Partington Aston and which Aston himself claimed entirely as his, is at least largely by Ainsworth. I am equally sure that *James the Second*, which was described on its first appearance in book form as "edited" by Ainsworth, is in fact his own work. On the other hand, *Modern Chivalry*, similarly labeled when it was published in *Ainsworth's Magazine*, is totally unlike anything else from Ainsworth's pen; and it is very probably the work of Mrs. Catherine Gore. By retaining *Sir John Chiverton* and *James the Second* and by rejecting *Modern Chivalry*, I establish the number of Ainsworth's novels as forty-one.

After the first chapter, my treatment of important facets of Ainsworth's work is based almost exclusively on evidence in his novels. I have quoted more copiously—particularly in Chapter 6, which is devoted to stylistic matters—than I would have done in treating a better-known writer or one whose books are more easily available. These quotations, I believe, convey the special flavor of his fiction better than any amount of commentary could do. Chapters 2 to 6 are very lightly footnoted, since it seemed more convenient to incorporate references parenthetically in the text. Because there is no standard edition of Ainsworth, these citations refer to the books (or parts) into which he ordinarily divided his novels and to chapters within those sections rather than to pages: large Roman numerals stand for sections; small Roman numerals, for chapters.

It would be absurd to claim that the purpose of a study like this is the rehabilitation of Ainsworth, for he can never again command the huge audience which devoured his books from *Rookwood* on into the 1840s. But he is too intriguing a novelist, one too closely connected with important tendencies in his own age and in ours, to be forgotten or condemned to a few careless and superficial sentences in histories of literature. He deserves to be read, with sympathy and discernment; and there is much in his best fiction to repay such reading. If this book stimulates some curious students of the novel to investigate *Rookwood*, or *Jack Sheppard*, or *The Tower of London*, or *Old Saint Paul's*, or any one of a dozen or more still very vital works of fiction, and if it helps them read this fiction with the requisite sympathy and discernment, I shall have achieved my main purpose.

GEORGE J. WORTH

The University of Kansas

ACKNOWLEDGMENTS

I owe thanks to the University of Kansas for supporting this study, at key stages, with grants from its General Research Fund and Graduate Research Fund. I am even more indebted to the University administration for recognizing that an English professor does not renounce scholarship when he becomes a departmental chairman and for providing me with the amount and kind of help that made it possible for me to work away steadily, though slowly, on this project through four busy and exciting years in the development of my Department.

In May, 1967, I read an early version of Chapter 4 to a meeting of English 399, our departmental colloquium for graduate students and faculty; and I profited much from that afternoon's discussion. My colleague Edwin M. Eigner has generously shared with me his wide range of knowledge and ideas about the nineteenth-century novel and Romantic fiction generally, and numerous other friends and students—more than I can remember and name—have contributed in one way or another, often merely by a chance remark, to the growth of this book.

G. J. W.

CONTENTS

CHRONOLOGY

1805   William Harrison Ainsworth born in Manchester, February 4.

1817   Enters the Manchester Free Grammar School.

1820   Begins writing plays.

1821   First appearance in print: *The Rivals: a Serio-Comic Tragedy*, published under the pseudonym "T. Hall" in the *Pocket Magazine*.

1822   Leaves the Grammar School. Begins the study of law. Dedicates his first book, pseudonymously published, to Lamb: *The Maid's Revenge; and A Summer's Evening Tale; with Other Poems*, "By Cheviot Ticheburn."

1824   After the death of his father, leaves Manchester for London to study law.

1826   Admitted as a qualified solicitor. Publication of *Sir John Chiverton* (in collaboration with J. P. Aston). Marries Anne Frances ("Fanny") Ebers, October 11.

1827   Birth of his first child, Fanny.

1829   Birth of his second child, Emily.

1830   Having abandoned publishing, begins the practice of law. Birth of his third child, Anne Blanche. Begins his association with the new *Fraser's Magazine*.

1834   *Rookwood*.

1835   Separation from his wife.

1837   *Crichton*.

1838   Death of his wife, March 6.

1839   *Jack Sheppard*. In March, becomes editor of *Bentley's Miscellany*.

1840   *The Tower of London;* begins serial publication of *Guy Fawkes*.

1841   *Guy Fawkes. Old Saint Paul's*. In December, resigns editorship of *Bentley's Miscellany*.

1842 Inception of *Ainsworth's Magazine*, February. *The Miser's Daughter*. Begins serial publication of *Windsor Castle*.

1843 *Windsor Castle*.

1844 *Saint James's*. Begins serial publication of *Auriol*, under the title of *Revelations of London*.

1845 Purchases the *New Monthly Magazine*, in June.

1847 Serial publication of *James the Second*.

1848 *James the Second*. Serial publication of *The Lancashire Witches*.

1849 *The Lancashire Witches*.

1851 Begins publication in parts of *The Life and Adventures of Mervyn Clitheroe*.

1853 Serial publication of *The Star-Chamber*. Moves from London. Begins serial publication of *The Flitch of Bacon*.

1854 *The Star-Chamber*. *The Flitch of Bacon*. Purchases *Bentley's Miscellany*. *Ainsworth's Magazine* ceases publication.

1855 Begins serial publication of *The Spendthrift*. *Ballads*.

1857 *The Spendthrift*.

1858 *Mervyn Clitheroe*.

1859 *The Combat of the Thirty*. Begins serial publication of *Ovingdean Grange*.

1860 *Ovingdean Grange*.

1861 *The Constable of the Tower*.

1862 *The Lord Mayor of London*. Begins serial publication of *Cardinal Pole*.

1863 *Cardinal Pole*. Begins serial publication of *John Law*.

1864 *John Law*. Begins serial publication of *The Spanish Match*, as *The House of Seven Chimneys*.

1865 *The Spanish Match*. *Auriol*. Begins serial publication of *The Constable de Bourbon*.

1866 *The Constable de Bourbon*. Begins serial publication of *Old Court*.

1867 *Old Court*. Begins serial publication of *Myddleton Pomfret*.

1868 *Myddleton Pomfret*. Sells *Bentley's Miscellany* back to Bentley. Serial publication of *The South-Sea Bubble*.

1869 Serial publication of *Hilary St. Ives*.

1870 *Hilary St. Ives*. Serial publication of *Talbot Harland*. Resigns editorship of *New Monthly Magazine*.

1871 *Tower Hill*. *The South-Sea Bubble*. *Talbot Harland*.

1872 *Boscobel*.

1873   *The Good Old Times;* titled *The Manchester Rebels of the Fatal '45* in subsequent editions.

1874   *Merry England.* Serial publication of *The Goldsmith's Wife.*

1875   *The Goldsmith's Wife. Preston Fight.*

1876   *The Leaguer of Lathom. Chetwynd Calverley.*

1877   *The Fall of Somerset.*

1878   *Beatrice Tyldesley.*

1879   *Beau Nash.*

1881   *Stanley Brereton.* Honored at a banquet in the Manchester Town Hall, September 15.

1882   Dies at Reigate, January 3. Buried at Kensal Green Cemetery.

CHAPTER 1

The Man and His Age

I *Biographical Sketch*

VERY few authors have been born into an environment as conducive to the nurture and growth of the qualities which make for success in literature as that in which William Harrison Ainsworth grew up. The place of his birth, on February 4, 1805, was Manchester—already, by nineteenth-century standards, a city; and one already deeply committed to the English industrial revolution. But it still retained much of its picturesqueness, and romantic associations with a colorful past were everywhere to be seen:

It abounded with whole streets of elaborately carved black-and-white timber houses, with quaintly-pointed gables and lattice-windows. In the outskirts of the town stood the ancient Halls of Hulme, Ordsall, Garrett, Irlam, and many another, reminiscent of the historic past; and not far from King Street was the beautiful Gothic Collegiate Church and the adjoining Chetham's College—that most fascinating of medieval buildings, with its quaint cloisters, monastic cells, baronial kitchen; its wealth of old oak furniture and panelling, and ancient books.[1]

King Street, where the family lived, was, in Ainsworth's boyhood, a "select, residential street of fine old Georgian houses, where many rich and influential citizens of Manchester still resided. . . . The flavour of the eighteenth century still hung about the street, and it had an old-world air" (I, 20–21).

Manchester was still so small as to put the surrounding countryside of Lancashire and Cheshire within fairly easy reach of all its inhabitants. That this countryside, too, was rich in historic associations Ainsworth—from an early age endowed with a strong curiosity about the past—was to learn in early boyhood. When he was six, his father bought a house, Beech Hill, in the Cheetham Hill district, two miles north of what was then the center of Manchester. There, while retaining

15

the King Street house as a winter residence, the family for many years spent its summers in "a rich, well-wooded country of undulating hills" (I, 28). After young Ainsworth entered the Manchester Free Grammar School—by far the city's oldest educational establishment, founded in 1515 by Hugh Oldham, Bishop of Exeter—at the age of twelve, he spent most of his school holidays in another rural setting, at Rostherne, Cheshire, at the house of his great-uncle, John Shuttleworth.

Books, stories, and writing were a part of Ainsworth's life almost literally from the beginning. His father, Thomas Ainsworth, a prominent lawyer and a member of a very old, illustrious Lancashire family, was something of an authority on criminal history. He was quite willing to regale his son with tales of highwaymen and with other exciting narratives; and young Harrison, who was keenly interested in such romantic stories, listened eagerly. Not unnaturally, he himself tried his hand at writing as soon as "he could first use a pen in earliest boyhood" (I, 27).

His literary imagination was additionally stimulated after 1817 by friendship with James Crossley, five years his senior, who came to Manchester in that year as an articled clerk in Thomas Ainsworth's law firm. Crossley was an omnivorous reader, an ardent book collector especially interested in antiquarian, historical, and archeological works and the Elizabethan and Jacobean poets and dramatists, and—much later—Thomas Ainsworth's partner. The clerk and his employer's son soon discovered their common interests and began an association which endured for sixty-five years. Whenever Ainsworth had an idea involving knowledge of the past, he could always, even in his old age, turn to Crossley for advice and information.

While Ainsworth was a student at the Grammar School, between 1817 and 1822, he began producing his own plays in a theater which he had set up in the basement of the family home on King Street. He built the stage machinery, made the properties and costumes, painted the scenery, and prepared the playbills by hand. Some of these plays were actually published in magazines, in whole or in part, and have survived in scattered copies; and it is possible to see in this youthful work more than a hint of his later melodramatic and Gothic style. The plays abound in passionate, high-flown speeches and in "the terrible, the mysterious, and the supernatural, combined with a minute description of scenery, buildings, and costumes" (I, 59—60).

Always a highly prolific writer, Ainsworth also during these years contributed a spate of material in other forms—original stories, poems, and essays, and translations from the Classics—to several popular magazines of the day: the *Pocket Magazine*, the *Edinburgh Magazine*, the *New Monthly Magazine*, the *European Magazine*, and the *London Magazine*. But, although literature might do very well as a hobby, a respectable young man had to have a profession; and for a successful lawyer's son the choice was obvious. On leaving school in 1822, Harrison Ainsworth became an articled clerk to Alexander Kay, solicitor and conveyancer, of Manchester; and thus, in keeping with his father's wishes, he began preparing himself for a career in the law.

But his true interests lay elsewhere. A handsome, gregarious young man by this time, he devoted himself more energetically than he probably should have to conviviality; and all the while the magnet of literature continued to draw him. He published a book of poems pseudonymously during the summer of 1822, which he dedicated to Charles Lamb, a fellow-contributor to the *London Magazine*, with whom he had struck up a friendship by correspondence. On March 20, 1824, he made the first of his several ventures into magazine editing and publishing: on that date he brought out the *Boeotian*, largely filled with his own work; but the little periodical expired after only six numbers. He also collaborated with a young clerk in his father's office, a fellow-alumnus of the Free Grammar School, one John Partington Aston, on a long romance which was not published until 1826, *Sir John Chiverton*.

This first, rather idyllic, phase of his young manhood came to an abrupt end with the death of Thomas Ainsworth on June 20, 1824. Since greater responsibilities in his father's firm would now devolve on Harrison, he determined to go to London the following winter to continue his study of law. There is no evidence that Ainsworth was not serious in his intention but, ironically, that decision to leave Manchester for the capital was the beginning of the end of his professional commitment to his father's calling. Though he devoted himself dutifully to his legal studies in London and was admitted as a qualified solicitor in the Court of King's Bench in 1826, Ainsworth found much else to occupy his time. Already something of a dandy, he led an active social life. He associated with writers, and continued writing himself. One of his new friends was John Ebers, who numbered publishing among the several enterprises in which he was engaged. Ainsworth, who went to work for Ebers in 1826, married his beautiful daughter Fanny the same year.

Also in 1826, Ebers brought out several of Ainsworth's works, most notably *Sir John Chiverton*. Though it must be rated a piece of juvenilia and is not often referred to in the pages that follow, *Sir John Chiverton* contains many distinctively Ainsworthian features and resembles much of his later work in being inspired by an actual structure rich in Gothic possibilities: Hulme Hall, on the outskirts of Manchester, which appears in the novel as Chiverton Hall. *Sir John Chiverton* was well received, and Ainsworth was especially pleased that it was taken note of by his literary hero, Sir Walter Scott, who read it, liked it, and asked to meet its author.

It surely did not take much pleading on Ebers's part to persuade Ainsworth, at about this time, to give up the law altogether and to manage the publishing end of Ebers's bookselling and circulating library business. At first, Ainsworth was quite successful in his new career, which brought him into contact with many famous writers. But he soon grew impatient with the restrictions of business life and abandoned this second profession within two years to return, temporarily, to his original one. He began practicing law in 1830 in London; and, though he kept up his practice, in a manner of speaking, until after the publication of *Rookwood* in 1834 and the great success which that novel brought him, he threw only a portion of his prodigious energy into his legal pursuits. He spent much time in travel and continued his writing and his association with men of letters, most notably the brilliant group which started *Fraser's Magazine* in 1830. Ainsworth wrote for it in its early years and, more significantly, began working in 1831 on his first mature novel, *Rookwood,* again stimulated by a strange old house, Cuckfield Place in Sussex, the residence of his friend William Sergison, which he was to turn into the gloomy Rookwood Place.

When the novel was published in three volumes by Richard Bentley in April, 1834, it instantly made Ainsworth's fame, selling prodigiously well and going through five large editions in three years. Perhaps the most telling sign of Ainsworth's sudden renown was his acceptance at this time into the two leading salons of London society, those of Lady Blessington and of Lord and Lady Holland, where the rich, the famous, and the powerful congregated. An attractive, stunningly dressed young man who had conquered literary London with *Rookwood,* Ainsworth was quite capable of holding up his head in such glittering company.

Personal misfortune, however, as much as financial success, necessitated a change in Ainsworth's domestic arrangements the following year. For reasons that are now considerably less than clear, Fanny left Ainsworth to return to her father (she died in 1838); and Ainsworth went to live at Kensal Lodge, a house on the Harrow Road in what was then country west of London. There, and in the adjoining Kensal

Manor House, to which he moved in March, 1841, he established himself as the most noted literary host of the time, entertaining lavishly and providing a rendezvous for countless gifted young writers, including, among many others, Dickens, Thackeray, and Disraeli.

It may help to establish Ainsworth's literary position in the 1830s to say a word about his connection with Charles Dickens. The first point to be made is that, when Ainsworth scored his triumph with *Rookwood* in 1834, Dickens was an unknown journalist. Ainsworth introduced Dickens to his first publisher, John Macrone, who published *Sketches by Boz,* his first book, in 1836, and to George Cruikshank, the illustrator of the *Sketches* and of *Oliver Twist.* Dickens met John Forster, who was to become his closest friend, most trusted adviser, and first real biographer, at Kensal Lodge; and, on a trip to Manchester with Dickens, Ainsworth introduced him to the benevolent merchants whom Dickens transformed into the Cheeryble brothers of his *Nicholas Nickleby.* It is clear, then, that Dickens was much in Ainsworth's debt. The two men remained good friends during most of Ainsworth's Harrow Road period; but, later, after Dickens's place as England's leading novelist was beyond question and Ainsworth's own fame and fortune had declined steeply, they understandably grew apart.

That fame and fortune reached its very considerable peak in the late 1830s and early 1840s. *Rookwood* was followed in 1837 by *Crichton,* which, like its predecessor, had an enormous sale. Effective as it was, however, this copiously documented historical tale of intrigue and romance at the French court in the sixteenth century lacked the broad appeal of the earlier novel, with its Gothic sensationalism and its glamorous highwayman-hero Dick Turpin; and, aware of this lack, Ainsworth resolved to return to the criminal sphere in his next work, *Jack Sheppard.* First published in *Bentley's Miscellany* as a serial between January, 1839, and February, 1840, and in three volumes by Bentley in October, 1839, *Jack Sheppard* scored another phenomenal success, outstripping *Crichton* and probably *Rookwood* as well. Numerous imitations and parodies of *Jack Sheppard* appeared almost at once, a sure sign of popular acceptance in those days, and eight different dramatic versions were produced in London, virtually simultaneously, in the autumn of 1839. The novel also aroused a very different response: a vigorous outcry concerning its alleged glorification of crime and immorality and the baneful effect which it was bound to have on the young and impressionable.[2]

While *Jack Sheppard* was running in *Bentley's Miscellany,* Ainsworth succeeded Dickens as editor of that periodical in March, 1839; and he began working at an even higher pitch of activity than he had been. The years 1840 and 1841 were perhaps the busiest, most productive of Ainsworth's exceedingly busy and productive life. In addition to his editorial duties, which he took very seriously indeed, he was occupied with three major novels: *The Tower of London,* which appeared in monthly parts from January through December, 1840; *Guy Fawkes* which ran as a serial in *Bentley's Miscellany* from January, 1840, through November, 1841; and *Old Saint Paul's,* which was published in the *Sunday Times* in weekly installments from January 3, 1841, through December 26 of the same year. All three novels are among his major, most enduring achievements.

Though, as a glance at the Chronology and a reading of the body of this book indicate, Ainsworth still had much good work, some of it even distinguished, to do, his career after 1842 seems to start its downward course. That he had begun to write himself out is possible; what seems more certain is that he devoted too much of his time to editing. Though he gave up *Bentley's Miscellany* in 1841, he started *Ainsworth's Magazine* the following February and purchased the *New Monthly Magazine* in 1845. He edited both periodicals until 1854, in which year he terminated *Ainsworth's* but again purchased *Bentley's,* so that he still retained responsibility for two magazines. This responsibility continued until he sold *Bentley's* in 1868. Aside from his editorial labors, which involved much reading of manuscripts and voluminous correspondence with contributors and would-be contributors, Ainsworth continued his own copious writing, doing much of the principal fiction in his magazines (beginning with the first installment of *The Miser's Daughter* in the initial number of *Ainsworth's*) as well as turning out many reviews and articles.

In 1853, Ainsworth left Kensal Manor Lodge and London to reside in Brighton, on England's south coast. Though he continued to edit his magazines and write books, and though he made frequent visits to London, this move clearly marked the end of the most important phase of his life. Nearly fifty years old and well past his first fame, he was no longer either the literary and social lion of London or the open-handed host to its preeminent men of letters. He had used a large part of his financial resources in splendid entertaining and countless acts of generosity, his books were not bringing in money as they once did, and his magazines had ceased to earn him much income. A new literary generation had usurped the high place he had once held: Dickens and Thackeray, men he had befriended when he was famous and they were unknown, were the leading novelists of the day; and the kind of fiction he knew best how to write—Gothic, historical, and rogue—had fallen from public favor, succeeded by a new kind of domestic realism focusing on contemporary and near-contemporary materials. It was this sort of novel which, in a very few years' time, was to make the fame of Anthony Trollope and George Eliot.

Though Ainsworth had another twenty-nine years to live and write, and though much of what he wrote needs to be discussed—if not always favorably—later in this book, little else remains to be recorded of his activities; and most of that has a kind of sad finality about it. In 1856, Lord Palmerston's government awarded him a Civil List pension of one hundred pounds a year—the characteristic tribute by a nation to a writer who has ceased to be a writer primarily and has become a monument. What little entertaining of his old friends he had been able to manage ceased in 1867 when he moved from Brighton to Tunbridge Wells. Bit by bit, to keep himself in funds, he sold the family property, beginning with the house in King Street and Beech Hill. *Bentley's Miscellany* was sold in 1868; the *New Monthly,* in 1870.

Ainsworth even had trouble finding good publishers: some of his later novels are so scarce today because they were published in cheap paperback editions by a man called Dicks, in whose penny weekly magazine *Bow Bells* they first appeared. A pathetic story told by Percy Fitzgerald and printed by Ellis gives some indication of the obscurity in which Ainsworth lived out the last twenty-odd years of his life:

"I recall a dinner at Teddington, in the sixties, given by Frederic Chapman, the publisher, at which were Forster and Browning. The latter said humorously, 'a sad, forlorn-looking being stopped me to-day and reminded me of old times. He presently resolved himself into—whom do you think?—Harrison Ainsworth!' " (II, 264)

The last of his many moves, to Reigate, took place in 1878; there he lived a solitary existence with a second wife of whom almost nothing is known.

Ainsworth's last flicker of glory—and it too has its element of pathos—came on September 15, 1881, when the Lord Mayor of Manchester gave a dinner in his honor at the Town Hall. All of Manchester's prominent citizens were there, but what was Ainsworth, whose own generation except for the faithful Crossley was dead and gone, to make of these youngsters? The sad, resigned face, fringed by receding white hair and a white beard, which stares off into space from the front page of the souvenir brochure of the dinner bears no recognizable relationship to the handsome young man whose picture was drawn by Maclise and D'Orsay in the 1820s and 1830s.

Three and a half months after the banquet, William Harrison Ainsworth was dead.

II *The Novel-Reading Audience in the Early Nineteenth Century*

As long as there has been prose fiction in England—certainly since Samuel Richardson and Henry Fielding began fashioning the classical novel as we know it in the 1740s—it has commanded a large and devoted audience. This audience grew steadily throughout the eighteenth century, stimulated by a variety of social, economic, and literary causes which cannot be treated here.[3] One phenomenon, however, that should be mentioned is the establishment, about 1790, of the Minerva Press by one William Lane in Leadenhall Street, London, which disseminated countless thousands of sentimental and sensational novels all over the country.

The status of the novel as the nineteenth century opened was not high. Largely because of the trash which the Minerva Press was purveying, the reading of prose fiction was considered an idle and frivolous, if not a downright immoral, occupation. As a result, "every novel came into the world with a brand upon it. The trail of the Minerva Press was over all. . . . To the largest part of the reading public . . . the novel, like the pole-cat, was known only by name and a reputation for bad odour."[4] It is not surprising, then, that, by and large, the most considerable authors at the beginning of the century—like the major Romantics, for example—shunned the novel, devoting themselves instead to poetry and, to a lesser extent, drama, even when they wanted to work on a large scale. Most writers of novels in the early years of the new century were women; and their productions were, on the whole, distinctly lightweight. The exception is, of course, Jane Austen; but she was virtually unknown until a few years before her death in 1817.[5]

Nevertheless, forces were at work during these years which created the enthusiastic reading public for fiction which existed by the second quarter of the century. Because this was the audience to which Ainsworth—and, later, Dickens, Thackeray, and their illustrious contemporaries—catered, a few words should be said about it. Indeed, much in Ainsworth's novels that seems to us puzzling or annoying can be understood only if we know something of the size, the composition, and the tastes of the public which he was clearly anxious to please.

In the first place, the size of this audience, or potential audience, increased remarkably between, say, 1800 and 1850. It is not enough to point to statistics, like the doubling of population in England and Wales during the first half of the century;[6] what is much more relevant is that there is every reason to believe that at least a comparable growth, both in absolute numbers and in proportion to the rest of the population, took place in the novel-reading middle and lower middle classes.

Though there are some individual bits of evidence to the contrary, it is doubtful that the working classes provided many readers for serious fiction since real literacy was not yet very widespread among them. Such elementary education as there was, largely provided by a crazy-quilt of inadequately run and indifferently staffed dame schools, charity schools, factory schools, workhouse schools, "ragged schools," and Sunday schools, can have done little to whet the taste for reading of a poor child living in unimaginable squalor. The state played no role in education before 1833; and private philanthropic agencies, both religious and secular, which sought to bring learning to the poor emphatically scorned reading for pleasure. In an age when the average working day, six days a week, was fourteen to sixteen hours, there was little leisure for books; and, even when a bit of time could be snatched, there was, in the slum which the ordinary laborer called home, little privacy, less light, and no comfort for novel reading.

Still, there were readers, more and more of them, in the rapidly growing urban proletariat, but neither their tastes nor their financial position allowed most of them a place in the public on which the major novelists and the orthodox publishers had their eye. This fact is attested to by the existence, as early as the 1820s, of a vast and highly successful publishing underground dealing chiefly in very cheap issues of a sub-literature of crime and sensation and of piracies and plagiarisms of work by popular authors. "What Ainsworth brought to the drawing-room audience, the hacks of Salisbury Square manufactured for the tenements." [7]

It is mainly to the "drawing-room," rather than to the "tenements," that we must look in our assessment of the novel-reading audience of the first half of the nineteenth century. Though statistics are, naturally, impossible to come by (how, after all, can we enumerate such a phenomenon as a reading audience or, worse yet, a potential reading audience?), it is clear that the growth of a class with the education, the leisure, the taste, the means, and indeed the need to read must have been at least as rapid as the growth of the population as a whole. Just as the industrial revolution demanded an ever-increasing army of operatives for its machines, so it required another, though smaller, army of managers, supervisors, and clerks to keep the machines and their operatives functioning smoothly. As commerce grew, so did the need for merchants, bankers, lawyers, and accountants. And a rapidly expanding society required the services of more doctors, more clergymen, more army and naval officers, more government functionaries. For their wives and daughters, life was much easier than it had been, and there was more free time for reading than could have been spared a generation or two earlier. Servants were readily available and did not demand unreasonable wages. The increasing prevalence of cheap manufactured and processed goods, including such domestic items as soap, candles, cloth, and food products, lightened many household tasks and did away altogether with the need for others.

In the search for leisure pursuits, the members of the early nineteenth-century middle class were severely restricted. Not only was there no cinema, no radio, no television, no recorded music, but the numerous adherents of evangelical religion were severely discouraged from indulging in such amusements of the day as the theater, the music hall, dancing, or card playing. Small wonder that not only reading but reading aloud in the family circle formed a chief mode of polite recreation throughout the century. For consumption under such circumstances by such an audience, novelists had to produce work that was morally and intellectually edifying as well as entertaining. It is tempting to speculate on how many scores of thousands of Victorian readers who had had very little formal schooling learned by their firesides much of what they knew of the English past from Ainsworth's historical fiction.

The prices charged for new novels were prohibitive by nineteenth-century standards. Thirty-one shillings and sixpence was the standard price for a three-volume set from the early 1820s on, a sum which was equivalent to the average weekly salary of a clerk or a skilled worker. Normally, therefore, readers obtained such novels from circulating libraries, of which there were many, rather than from retail booksellers. For an annual fee of two guineas, they could borrow from one of these lending establishments all the new books they could read. Because the circulating libraries provided such a large share of the market for new fiction, they exerted a powerful though subtle pressure on publishers; and, because their standards were notoriously conservative, they effectively prevented the appearance of novels with questionable tendencies. A novelist like Ainsworth, who appealed to a large audience, therefore had to guard himself against "impropriety" and to maintain an acceptably didactic tone in his work.

Two other modes of publication—both, like the three-volume novel, resorted to by Ainsworth—were common in the first half of the nineteenth century: the issuing of a novel in successive monthly numbers costing a shilling each, which became especially popular after the great success of Dickens's *Pickwick Papers* in 1836–37; and magazine serialization, which cost the reader more than monthly parts published separately but which still constituted a saving over the purchase of a new novel in three volumes. For the middle-class reader, such devices helped to make new novels more accessible; but, for the novelist, writing fiction in installments, like the quasi-censorship of the circulating libraries, created artistic problems involving the plot arrangement rather than the selection or handling of subject matter. In order to create the kind of suspense that would make the public eager to buy the next month's number (and thereby generate greater royalties), the author usually felt compelled to end each installment at some crucial point.

Also catering to this enlarged audience was a steady stream of new periodicals with considerable intellectual pretensions. Though they did relatively little with fiction, especially at the beginning, they were widely circulated among serious readers and doubtless served to raise the level of literary taste. Among the more important of these may be mentioned the *Edinburgh Review* (founded 1802), the *Quarterly Review* (1809), the *Literary Gazette* and *Blackwood's Edinburgh Magazine* (both 1817), the *London Magazine* (1820), the *Spectator* and the *Athenaeum* (both 1828), and *Fraser's Magazine* (1830).

But something more was needed to create the large and devoted novel-reading audience for which Ainsworth wrote, and that something began in 1814 when Sir Walter Scott published his first novel, *Waverley*. It was an immediate success, and so were the other novels by Scott which followed it, usually at the rate of one or two a year, for more than a decade and a half. Their sales, by early nineteenth-century standards, were most impressive: the first edition of *Waverley*, consisting of one thousand copies, was sold out in five weeks; a total of six thousand copies was sold in six months. Two thousand copies of *Guy Mannering* (1815) were bought by eager readers the day after publication. Six thousand copies of *The Antiquary* (1816) were sold within six days of its appearance and ten thousand copies of *Rob Roy*

(1818) were sold within a fortnight. Such successes were not ephemeral: between 1829 and 1849 the Waverley Novels sold 78,270 sets, in addition to scores of thousands of copies of individual novels.[8]

Sales statistics like these, however, are much less important than the telling impact which Scott made on the reading public in the second and third decades of the century and the profound changes which he wrought in the makeup of that audience. He enlarged the public for novels, to be sure; but, more significantly, he brought into it readers who had previously disdained the novel. Nineteenth-century memoirs and letters are full of testimonials to this effect, but we may content ourselves with a quotation from Mrs. Kitty Cuthbertson, herself a Minerva Press author:

The whole world, from the learned heads of universities to the ragged pupils of our national schools, consume their leisure hours in reading the works of one prolific novelist; he who supersedes the pursuit of old black letter literature; he from whose heroines our fair ones form their manners; he whose muse supplies the patriot with strains for melodies to whet their courage and their sword. And who can dare to enter the lists, even to seek for food, where such a mighty warrior rides triumphant? nay, now rides, like Phoebus, in his daily race alone.[9]

What was it Scott had done to set himself apart from his immediate predecessors and contemporaries? It is difficult to give a succinct answer, but we may point to the fact that, eschewing sentimentalism and sensationalism, Scott had peopled his novels with credible men and women confronting genuine problems and operating in realistic settings; that he had faced moral issues squarely and sensibly, without preaching and without flinching; that he had diffused his own rich humanity and no less rich humor throughout his narratives. His characteristics as a historical novelist are more fully treated in the next section of this chapter. But one thing is certain: by creating a public for the novel, Scott made possible nineteenth-century fiction as we know it.

Dickens was the first major writer after Scott to take advantage of this new readership; but, even before the publication of *Pickwick*, Ainsworth aroused its enthusiasm with *Rookwood* in 1834. It seems reasonable to suggest that Ainsworth owed his initial fame to an accident of chronology, since he had the good fortune to find the right sort of ready-made audience for his fiction during the interregnum between the death of Scott in 1832 and Dickens's debut as a novelist in 1836–37. But more than mere chronology was involved in determining the particular mode of Ainsworth's success: when he emerged as a novelist, he was in a unique position to avail himself of three important literary traditions which were either at or just past their peak: those of the historical novel, the Gothic novel, and the rogue novel.

Because Ainsworth made significant contributions to all three types of novel, it is worth our while to examine each in some detail. Only by doing so may we assess the extent and value of what he did with them. He also reacted against a fourth tradition, a dying one, that of the fashionable novel, while nevertheless incorporating elements of it into his later work. And—no doubt unconsciously—Ainsworth went outside the novel altogether in borrowing for use in his fiction many melodramatic devices of the theater of his day. These forces shaping his art also need to be considered if we are to understand his work fully.

III *Literary Influences: The Historical Novel*

There is little reason to doubt that, without the overwhelming example of Scott, Ainsworth would have written a different kind of fiction. Scott himself recognized *Sir John Chiverton,* Ainsworth's first sustained narrative, as derived from his own practice;[10] and, by the time Ainsworth had devoted himself fully to novel-writing in the 1830s, historical fiction on the general lines laid down by Scott had established itself as one of the dominant literary modes. But Scott did not invent the historical novel; rather, he took a mode of fiction which was more than two centuries old and gave it a form and a substance which it had never previously had. As Sir John Marriott wrote: "The historical novels written before 1814 may be regarded as preparing the way for the advent of Scott. Those that have been written since look back to him with filial piety."[11] To grasp the meaning of Marriott's assertion is to gain a richer understanding of the historical fiction of Ainsworth, one of Scott's first followers but by no means his slavish imitator.

A kind of historical fiction was being produced in England as early as the reign of Elizabeth I, but not until the nineteenth century did the form combine artistic effectiveness and historical accuracy in the manner of Scott and Ainsworth. Thomas Nashe's *The Unfortunate Traveller, or The Life of Jack Wilton* (1594), which has been called "the first historical novel,"[12] is in fact primarily a picaresque story. However, it happens to be set in the time of Henry VIII, eighty years before the composition of the novel; and Nashe made some attempt to achieve accuracy in his depiction of life in Henry's time. By contrast, Thomas Deloney's *The Pleasant History of John Winchcomb, in His Younger Years Called Jack of Newbury* (1597), which dealt with the same period, was much less concerned with historical verisimilitude and constantly sought to relate the matter and the message of the narrative to the author's own day.

Over a century later, Daniel Defoe, who was always trying to pass off fiction as fact, turned out the *Memoirs of a Cavalier* (1720), purporting to be a firsthand record of the English Civil War, and *A Journal of the Plague Year* (1722), the account in diary form of a fictitious saddler's experiences during the great London pestilence of 1665. It is worth noting that Ainsworth used both the *Journal* and Defoe's pamphlet *Due Preparations for the Plague* in writing his own fictional narrative of that terrible visitation, *Old Saint Paul's.*[13]

A later candidate for the title of "the first English historical novel" is *Longsword, Earl of Salisbury, an Historical Romance* (1762),[14] anonymously published but now generally attributed to John Leland. The action of the novel, which takes place in the late twelfth and early thirteenth centuries, involves some historical figures; but Leland gives notice in the preface that he will not necessarily be confined by documentary sources. This statement is a classic one testifying to the casualness with which earlier novelists regarded the historical record—a casualness against which both Scott and Ainsworth later reacted:

THE out-lines of the following story, and some of the incidents and more minute circumstances, are to be found in the antient English historians. If too great liberties have been taken in altering or enlarging their accounts, the reader who looks only for amusement will probably forgive it: the learned and critical (if this work should be honoured by such readers) will deem it a matter of too little consequence to call for the severity of their censure.

The suggestion that "the learned and critical" will not take the book seriously gives a good indication of the low status of the novel a half-century before *Waverley*.

Two years after *Longsword* came Horace Walpole's *The Castle of Otranto*, supposedly also set in the Middle Ages, but showing even less connection with a specific time and place. Like later eighteenth-century novels dealing with the past—such as Clara Reeve's *The Old English Baron* (1778), Sophia Lee's *The Recess, or a Tale of Other Times* (1785), Ann Radcliffe's *The Castles of Athlin and Dunbayne* (1789), and the same author's *The Mysteries of Udolpho* (1794)—*The Castle of Otranto* exploits a vaguely antique and exotic locale to arouse Gothic shudders, and a real sense of history is almost entirely missing. Much closer to Scott in spirit as well as in time was Jane Porter's *The Scottish Chiefs* (1810), whose protagonist was the great Scottish hero Sir William Wallace and which gave a reasonably accurate picture of a stirring episode of the country's history.

As for Scott himself, it must not be assumed that chauvinism was the predominant element in his appeal. Far from it: his taking such a line would have severely restricted his success with English readers, and his phenomenal popularity south of the Tweed is a matter of record. Nor was Scott unduly wistful about the vanished glories of Scotland's past. Much that was good, noble, and beautiful had disappeared, to be sure, as feudalism, nationalism, and Scottish political integrity were swallowed up in the union with England; but the world had moved forward, and it behooved practical, realistic men and women to move along with it. Historical change often involves heartbreak, but man must accommodate himself to it and make the best of it, recognizing that progress has a bright as well as a cold, grim side. This message, coming at the beginning of what everyone regarded as a revolutionary age, had its relevance for others than Scotsmen. Muted and somewhat simplified, it appears often in the historical novels of Ainsworth, though he tended to be rather more dogged and unbending than Scott in his attachment to lost causes.

Combining nostalgia for the past with acceptance of the present, Scott ranged freely backward and forward through Scottish and English history, basing his fiction more solidly on recorded fact than any of his predecessors had done. What was more important, however, was his ability to capture and transmit the *spirit* of the times and the places he depicted—a knack which Ainsworth did not master nearly so well, and for which he tried to compensate by copious borrowing from chroniclers and historians and by the use of archaic language.

Scott had many followers. Aside from Ainsworth himself, we may note, first of all, George Croly, whose *Salathiel* (1829) dealt with the destruction of Jerusalem by the Romans under Titus. More important, because much more prolific, was G. P. R. James, author of seventy-seven works in 198 volumes, most of them historical novels. His first was *Richelieu* (1829); its most notable successors were *Darnley* (1830), *De L'Orme* (1830), *Philip Augustus* (1831), *Henry Masterton* (1832), *Morley Ernstein* (1842), and *Agnes Sorel* (1853). Edward Bulwer-Lytton* was always highly responsive to literary fashions, and his

---

* I call him by that name, which he did not assume in full until 1843, in this book. At the beginning of his career, he was known as Edward Lytton Bulwer.

turning to historical fiction in such novels as *The Last Days of Pompeii* (1834), *Rienzi* (1835), *The Last of the Barons* (1843), and *Harold* (1848) may safely be regarded as a sign of the great popularity of the form in the 1830s and 1840s. Even Dickens tried his hand at it in *Barnaby Rudge* (1841), partly set at the time of the Gordon Riots of 1780; though the novel has its staunch defenders, it is generally considered one of Dickens's weaker efforts.

Though the historical novel has endured as a subspecies down to our own day and has enjoyed frequent periods of revival, interest in that mode of fiction seems to have declined quite seriously in England after the 1840s. Historical novels by very estimable writers—for example, Thackeray's *Henry Esmond* (1852), Charles Kingsley's *Westward Ho!* (1855), Dickens's *A Tale of Two Cities* (1859), Reade's *The Cloister and the Hearth* (1861), and George Eliot's *Romola* (1862—63)—continued, of course, to be published; but these in general were not representative productions of their authors, and it was no longer possible to make one's fortune solely or chiefly as a historical novelist. Trollope, who had unsuccessfully attempted the form with *La Vendée* (1850), was received with the following words when he arrived, a few years later, at his publisher's office with a new manuscript under his arm: "I hope it's not historical, Mr. Trollope? Whatever you do, don't be historical; your historical novel is not worth a damn." [15]

Ainsworth himself, however, went on producing historical novels four decades after such fiction began to go out of style. To be sure, by this time he had largely lost his hold on readers, who were now interested in other things; but he was not able, either, to capture their fancy with more modish novels. Perhaps inspired by such first-person narratives as Charlotte Brontë's *Jane Eyre* (1847), Dickens's *David Copperfield* (1849—50), and Thackeray's *Pendennis* (1848—50), as Ellis suggests (II, 177), Ainsworth began issuing the semi-autobiographical *Mervyn Clitheroe* in monthly parts in December, 1851. But, when the public did not take to it, Ainsworth stopped after the fourth number, not to resume until December, 1857. His next venture into contemporary subject matter did not come until 1866, when he began running *Old Court* in *Bentley's Miscellany*; but this novel and its four non-historical successors—*Myddleton Pomfret* (1868), *Hilary St. Ives* (1870), *Chetwynd Calverley* (1876), and *Stanley Brereton* (1881)—must be counted among Ainsworth's weakest creations. It is not too much to say that Ainsworth's great success was closely linked with the vogue of the historical novel and that, when this kind of fiction ceased to be fashionable, Ainsworth—who was too old, too written-out, or too much the slave of habit to change—also went out of style.

IV *Literary Influences: The Gothic Novel*

In the preface to *Rookwood* that Ainsworth wrote for an 1849 edition, he stated that his literary mission at the outset of his career as a novelist had been to bring about the revival of "old Romance" as practiced in the two generations just before his own "by Horace Walpole, Monk Lewis, Mrs. Radcliffe, and Maturin." It is to the kind of fiction—commonly referred to as the Gothic novel—written by these authors, their contemporaries, and their successors, that we must look next in our attempt to place Ainsworth within the traditions he pursued.

For many years prior to the second half of the eighteenth century, "Gothic" had been a term of reproach in England, suggesting barbarous rudeness as opposed to classical balance, learning, politeness, and restraint. It was Bishop Richard Hurd, in his *Letters on Chivalry and Romance* (1762), who first made a plea for "Gothic Chivalry" and "Gothic Romance" as worthy of serious consideration; and this pleading came as part of a great revival of interest in the early literature and pre-literature of the English, the Scots, and kindred peoples. Some of the landmarks in this revival were the poetry of James Macpherson and Thomas Chatterton, some of the work of Thomas Gray, Thomas Percy's collection *Reliques of Ancient English Poetry* (1765), and Thomas Warton's *History of English Poetry* (1774–81).

Gothicism first invaded English fiction in *The Castle of Otranto* (1764), by Horace Walpole, a wealthy and talented amateur of letters, who had built himself an elaborate little pseudo-Gothic castle, Strawberry Hill, at Twickenham, near London. Very short as eighteenty-century novels went, *The Castle of Otranto* was a tale of mystery, intrigue, and supernatural horror, crudely put together and set in a gloomy Italian structure which was an amalgam of Strawberry Hill and Trinity College, Cambridge. The novel was warmly received in its own day and continued to be read with admiration to the time of Sir Walter Scott, who wrote a very flattering introduction for a later edition. Scott, who called Walpole the pioneer in a "new species of literary composition," pointed in *The Castle of Otranto* to its "chastity and precision of style, to a happy combination of supernatural agency with human interest, to a tone of feudal manners and language, sustained by characters strongly drawn and well discriminated, and to unity of action producing scenes alternately of interest and of grandeur." [16]

An infinitely more skillful craftsman than Walpole, Scott was to make highly sophisticated use of many of the devices of *The Castle of Otranto*—suspense, thrilling adventures, romantic backgrounds—fifty years and more later; and thus he helped transmit the Gothic tradition to the nineteenth century. Between Walpole and Scott came dozens of other practitioners of the genre. Ann Radcliffe's *The Mysteries of Udolpho* (1794) and Matthew Gregory Lewis's *The Monk* (1796), written in imitation of *The Mysteries of Udolpho* but going considerably beyond Mrs. Radcliffe in its voluptuousness and in its unapologetic and unexplained supernaturalism, were perhaps the best-known Gothic novels. Among the many others written in the last quarter of the eighteenth century and the first quarter of the nineteenth are Sophia Lee's *The Recess* (1785); Mrs. Radcliffe's *The Castles of Athlin and Dunbayne* (1789), *A Sicilian Romance* (1790), *The Romance of the Forest* (1791), and *The Italian* (1794); Regina Maria Roche's *The Children of the Abbey* (1796); Charlotte Dacre's *Zafloya, or The Moor* (1806); Charles Robert Maturin's *The Fatal Revenge* (1807); Mary Shelley's *Frankenstein* (1818); and—possibly the last truly characteristic example of the kind—Maturin's *Melmoth the Wanderer* (1820). These novels are still of some interest.

Different though these romances are from one another, we can, without undue simplification, point to a number of typical features which most of them share: a prevailing atmosphere of terror and suspense; a copious use of supernatural agents and events; ominous prophecies; sensational deaths, murders, and suicides; strange, wild, gloomy landscapes; generalized, vague geography and equally generalized, anachronistic history; intense emotional fervor, usually involving interaction among a virtuous heroine, a stainless hero, and a deep-dyed villain. Most characteristic of all, however, is the setting of the Gothic novel:

the remote and ruined castle with its antique courts, deserted chambers, pictured windows that exclude the light, haunted galleries among whose mouldering gloom is heard the rustle of an unseen robe, a sigh, a hurried footfall where no mortal step should tread; the ancient manor, hidden away in the heart of a pathless forest, a home of memories of days long gone before when bright eyes glanced from casement and balcony over the rich domain, the huge-girthed oaks, the avenues and far-stretching vistas, the cool stream winding past the grassy lawns, but now tenanted only by a silver-headed retainer and his palsied dame; the huge fortress set high upon some spar of the Apennines, dark machicolated battlements and sullen towers which frown o'er the valleys below, a lair of masterless men, through whose dim corridors prowl armed bandits, whose halls ring with hideous revelry or anon are silent as the grave; the lone and secret convent amid the hills ruled by some proud abbess whose nod is law, a cloister of which the terraces overlook vast precipices shagged with larch and darkened by the gigantic pine, whose silences are only disturbed by the deep bell that tolls to midnight office and the ceremonies of solemn prayer.[17]

Ainsworth's *Sir John Chiverton* and *Rookwood,* his first two novels, written not long after the Gothic vogue was at its height, carry the tradition, virtually unchanged, into the second quarter of the century. But almost all of his later work, even that with contemporary subjects and including his last novel, *Stanley Brereton* (1881), is full of Gothic devices: ancient castles, ruined abbeys, haunted rooms, sliding panels, secret passages, and subterranean vaults are standard features of his settings; mystery, intrigue, and violence flourish; and many a character is lifted from the pages of one of his Gothic predecessors. We investigate this aspect of Ainsworth's work more fully in Chapter 4.

The Gothic strain in fiction seems to appeal to something basic in our nature; and, though the external trappings of the form have changed since the early days, it is still utilized. Certainly Gothic novels were written throughout the nineteenth century in England, despite changes of fashion in life and art, a point we can demonstrate without going beyond the fiction of Ainsworth. In his *Stanley Brereton,* there is a ghost and a brooding, oppressive sense of fate verging on the supernatural; but there are also such modern features as lawn tennis at the upper-middle-class country house, telegrams, cigarettes, easy divorce, excursions to the Crystal Palace, and holidays on the Riviera. Many of Ainsworth's contemporaries wrote Gothic novels of one kind or another, including such authors of best sellers as Bulwer-Lytton, G. W. M. Reynolds, and Mary Elizabeth Braddon. The Irish novelist Sheridan Le Fanu made remarkably effective use of the occult in such books as *The House by the Churchyard* (1861–62), *Wylder's Hand* (1863–64), *Uncle Silas* (1864), and *In a Glass Darkly* (1872). Charlotte Brontë in *Jane Eyre* and her sister Emily in *Wuthering Heights* employed Gothic devices, as did Dickens, Wilkie Collins, and Thomas Hardy in any number of their books. So did three American authors whose works were widely read in England in the nineteenth century: Edgar Allan Poe, Nathaniel Hawthorne, and Henry James. And, in our own age, we have only to think of William Faulkner as a novelist whose strength often derives from Gothic materials.

About Ainsworth himself it is fair to say that he began writing Gothic fiction, of a virtually unadulterated kind, when that species of novel was still enjoying its first vogue in a relatively pure state and that he continued to resort to Gothic features to the very end of his long career.

V *Literary Influences: The Rogue Novel*

As we have seen, Ainsworth owed much of his early popularity to the fact that he worked within two well established traditions, those of the historical novel and of the Gothic romance. The first of these achieved its greatest prestige with the work of Scott and his immediate successors, like Ainsworth; the second, though older, nevertheless retained much of its vitality into the 1820s and 1830s, and beyond. A third relevant tradition in fiction, that of the rogue novel or Newgate novel, did not reach its peak until the 1830s and 1840s; and two of Ainsworth's earliest and greatest successes, *Rookwood* and *Jack Sheppard*, had a major part in establishing its fame—or, perhaps it would be better to say, its notoriety.

Long before Ainsworth's day, of course, English literature had rather frequently dealt with the careers of figures who earned their living or their reputation by crime. As Frank W. Chandler made clear in his exhaustive study of the subject, "the literature of roguery" was a product "of the later Renaissance."[18] It was palatable to a large audience of generally, if not always enthusiastically, law-abiding and civilized people by virtue of the fact that "roguery" is not at all the same as "villainy": "The latter is the creature of malice, if not of pathological conditions; its evil proceeds to extremes. The former is less vicious; it regards rascality with humor, or explains it as the result of social environment."[19]

Born in England in the sixteenth century and practiced throughout the seventeenth, rogue literature flourished even more vigorously in the eighteenth, when "Newgate prison and the gallows, the ultimate enforcers of the law, hovered in the imagination of Englishmen" in a manner difficult to understand today.[20] Crime and the exploits of colorful criminals were the subjects of countless legends, and the public executions at Tyburn were among the most popular entertainments of the age.

Literature of all kinds and also the other arts made copious use of these materials. Collections of criminal biography, called "Newgate calendars," appeared from the early eighteenth century onward. Daniel

Defoe, to name but one prominent author, concerned himself at length and in considerable, almost loving, detail with fictitious malefactors in such novels as *Moll Flanders* (1722) and with real ones, including Jack Sheppard, in countless pamphlets. Ballad operas, most notably Gay's *The Beggar's Opera* (1728), were written about criminals, and the most famous domestic tragedy of the century, George Lillo's *The London Merchant* (1731), dealt with a young apprentice who is lured into a life of robbery and murder by a wicked woman. Many of William Hogarth's best-known pictures depict the London underworld; Hogarth himself appears as a character in *Jack Sheppard* and the parallels between that novel and Hogarth's series of twelve plates called "Industry and Idleness" (1747) have often been remarked upon.

But not until the nineteenth century, when novelists—as we have seen—wrote for a very large audience, did the Newgate novel make its greatest impact.[21] The reading public, which had hardly existed in any modern sense before, was no less susceptible than earlier generations had been to the pleasures of seeing roguery skillfully depicted in literature; and this epoch was very much aware of crime as a social problem in a way that would have been foreign to the eighteenth-century mind. Legal reformers were pointing to the inequities and the barbarity of English law, and sweeping changes in that legal non-system were undertaken during Sir Robert Peel's tenure of office as Home Secretary in the 1820s and on into the 1830s and early 1840s. At the same time, parliamentary committees and royal commissions, supported by the new science of statistics,[22] were bringing to general notice the social conditions which, it was increasingly felt, were responsible for the existence of crime.

The new rogue fiction of the 1830s and 1840s provoked a great deal of controversy, which—like comparable controversies today—surely did sales no harm. These novels were widely condemned for their violations of morality and good taste, for the immeasurable damage that might be done to impressionable readers by depicting a criminal as a human being rather than as a monster—possibly even an attractive human being or one who might arouse sympathy. They were published in an age which was far more self-consciously moralistic than those which had preceded it—an age, moreover, of tremendous political and social unrest and change. They were obviously addressed to a growing reading audience, drawn from an increasingly wide social base, about whose susceptibility to contamination by literature there was real worry.

The earliest practitioner of the nineteenth-century Newgate novel was Edward Bulwer-Lytton. Though he had made use of crime and criminals in his earlier fiction, it was not till *Paul Clifford* (1830) that these elements assumed a central position. It is the story of an eighteenth-century highwayman, the sort of criminal who would have had a prominent place in the Newgate calendars had he been real, who is transported to but escapes from an Australian penal colony and then becomes a respected citizen in North America. Bulwer-Lytton set the tone for a number of the novel's successors by carefully explaining how the potentially good nature of his protagonist was corrupted in childhood; even in Clifford's maturity, there are mitigating elements about his conduct.

The theme of social purpose and social reform is clearly present in *Paul Clifford,* as it is not in Bulwer-Lytton's next effort in the Newgate genre, *Eugene Aram* (1832). A murderer rather than a mere robber, and a scholar of some repute, Aram was an actual character in the Newgate calendars, but he is romanticized by Bulwer-Lytton into a tormented, tragic hero. *Eugene Aram* was even more popular than *Paul Clifford* had been, and it created even more acrimonious comment among the reviewers. *Fraser's Magazine,* for instance, was incensed: "We dislike altogether this awakening sympathy with interesting criminals, and wasting sensibilities on the scaffold and the gaol. It is a modern, a depraved, a corrupting taste." [23]

For better or worse, rogue novels were now attracting considerable attention, and it was probably as much owing to its Newgate as to its Gothic features that Ainsworth's *Rookwood* created such a sensation on its publication in 1834. The criminal underworld makes numerous appearances in *Rookwood,* most notably in the person of Dick Turpin, an actual Newgate denizen executed in 1739. Not altogether accurately, Turpin had long been known to a vast popular audience as the type of the romantic highwayman; and his rather contrived presence in the novel—he has virtually nothing to do with the main action—was immediately seized upon as a great virtue by the public, if not by the critics, of Ainsworth's day.

Certainly the greatest novelist to work in the Newgate tradition was Charles Dickens. Always keenly aware of social injustice and its close causal link with the prevalence of immorality and crime among the lower orders, Dickens made his two notable contributions to the Newgate novel in *Oliver Twist* (1838) and *Barnaby Rudge* (1841). Oliver's journey from the workhouse at the beginning to respectability and happiness at the end takes him, twice, to the den of thieves presided over by one of Dickens's most memorable creations, Fagin, who was based on a well-known London fence, Isaac (or Ikey) Solomon. A good part of *Barnaby Rudge*, in which Dickens's anger against a cruel social system and the unjust laws and barbarous punishments it fosters is even fiercer than in *Oliver Twist*, is set in Newgate prison itself, which is attacked and set afire during the course of the novel.

Ainsworth's second work in this form, *Jack Sheppard* (1839), had much in common with *Oliver Twist*. *Jack Sheppard* began running in *Bentley's Miscellany* as *Oliver Twist* was nearing its end there: for four months in 1839, the serializations of the two novels in the same magazine overlapped, both illustrated by George Cruikshank. Each author exposed a susceptible young boy to a criminal environment: Dickens's protagonist retained his virtue; Ainsworth's succumbed to temptation. Like Dickens, Ainsworth introduced a Jewish villain, a much feebler one than Fagin but resembling him in sporting the stage Jew's characteristic adornment, a red beard.

Again in the character Sheppard, as he had done in using Dick Turpin in *Rookwood*, Ainsworth depicted a well-known Newgate robber; and he peopled the new novel with numerous other characters, rather freely adapted, from criminal history and legend. The most notorious of these was Jonathan Wild, Jack's nemesis, an actual eighteenth-century gangster and informer who had himself been the protagonist of a famous novel nearly a hundred years earlier, Henry Fielding's satiric *Jonathan Wild* (1743).

Jack Sheppard soon became more popular than *Oliver Twist*—Keith Hollingsworth calls it "the high point of the Newgate novel as entertainment"[24]—and it may well have been that this popularity caused John Forster, by then Dickens's friend rather than Ainsworth's, to review *Jack Sheppard* as harshly as he did in the *Examiner*. But Forster was by no means alone in condemning the novel—which gave an often compassionate picture of Sheppard and which contained numerous scenes of violence, crime, and even sexual license—as a threat to public morals and decency. Indeed, not only Ainsworth's effort but the numerous adaptations which it inspired aroused much more controversy than any previous Newgate novel had done. Matters were not helped by the fact that the perpetrator of a notorious 1840 murder, one B. F. Courvoisier, a valet who killed his aged master, Lord William Russell, reportedly stated in one of his confessions that he got the idea for his brutal crime from reading *Jack Sheppard*.[25]

Whether for this reason or for other, unknown, ones, Ainsworth abandoned the rogue novel after *Jack Sheppard* and returned to historical fiction. He had planned to write a novel about another legendary highwayman, Claude Duval; but he never carried out his intention, though Duval does play a role, much later, in his *Talbot Harland* (1871). Bulwer-Lytton, on the other hand, had one more Newgate novel in him; he published *Lucretia, or The Children of Night* in 1846. The story dealt with a pair of cold-blooded murderers and it was inspired by the career of a notorious contemporary poisoner, Thomas Griffiths Wainewright. Like *Jack Sheppard, Lucretia* gave rise to a loud moralistic outcry, and it was succeeded by no more Newgate novels. The form seemed to be dead, though the public's interest in crime fiction remained very much alive; later in the century, however, and beginning very soon in the work of Dickens and Wilkie Collins, this interest shifted from the perpetrators to the victims and to the detectors of crime.

Among *Lucretia's* most vigorous critics was Thackeray, always a hostile critic of the Newgate novel and in particular of Bulwer-Lytton. In 1839-40 (while *Jack Sheppard* was appearing in the rival *Bentley's Miscellany*), Thackeray had published his *Catherine* in *Fraser's Magazine*. In doing so, he was attacking the excesses of the rogue novel by offering the public, his tongue in his cheek, a particularly outrageous example of the genre. He had freely adapted from one of the Newgate calendars, *The Malefactors' Bloody Register,* the story of Catherine Hayes, who had been burned alive at Tyburn in 1726 for having arranged a gruesome death for her husband. Though Thackeray's underlying moral intent, to show the evil consequence of glorifying criminals in fiction, was clear, his *Catherine* is full of parody directed against Newgate novels, chiefly those of Bulwer-Lytton.

Always intent on exposing and ridiculing what he took to be the literary follies and vices of the time, Thackeray continued his assaults against both Newgate fiction and Bulwer-Lytton in the pages of the infant *Punch* in the early and middle 1840s. Most notable among these sallies was "George de Barnwell" (1847), a mock retelling of George Lillo's eighteenth-century domestic tragedy, written in a cliché-ridden, high-flown style obviously reminiscent of the worst features of Bulwer-Lytton's prose. This attack so patently centered on *Eugene Aram,* which had been reissued in 1846, that Bulwer-Lytton thoroughly revised his novel before reissuing it again in 1849.

Thackeray's first and greatest masterpiece, *Vanity Fair,* which began appearing in the same year that saw the publication of "George de Barnwell," administered the *coup de grâce* to the Newgate novel by its burlesque of the excesses of such fiction. Always profoundly uneasy about his former friend Ainsworth's attraction to this sort of novel, Thackeray lampooned the storm scene in *Jack Sheppard* and the underworld "flash" jargon sprinkled throughout that novel and *Rookwood* in a passage, originally included in Chapter 6, which was omitted from *Vanity Fair* beginning with the edition of 1853:

The night was dark and wild—the clouds black—black—ink-black. The wild wind tore the chimney-pots from the roofs of the old houses and sent the tiles whirling and crashing through the desolate streets. No soul braved that tempest—the watchmen shrank into their boxes, whither the searching rain followed them—where the crashing thunderbolt fell and destroyed them—one had been so slain opposite the Foundling. A scorched gabardine, a shivered lantern, a staff rent in twain by the flash, were all that remained of stout Will Steadfast. A hackney-coachman had been blown off his coach-box, in Southampton Row—and whither? But the whirlwind tells no tidings of its victim, save his parting scream as he is borne onwards! Horrible night! It was dark, pitch dark; no moon, No, no. No moon, Not a star. Not a little feeble, twinkling, solitary star. There had been one at early evening, but he showed his face, shuddering, for a moment in the black heaven, and then retreated back.

One, two, three! It is the signal that Black Vizard had agreed on.

"Mofy! is that your snum?" said a voice from the area. "I'll gully the dag and bimbole the clicky in a snuffkin."

"Nuffle your clod, and beladdle your glumbanions," said Vizard, with a dreadful oath. "This way, men; if they screak, out with your snickers and slick! Look to the pewter room, Blowser. You, Mark, to the old gaff's mopus box! and I," added he, in a lower but more horrible voice, "I will look to Amelia!" 26

VI *Literary Influences: The Fashionable Novel*

Thackeray, in the original version of the same chapter of *Vanity Fair*, lampoons another mode of fiction popular in the second quarter of the nineteenth century: "the genteel rose-water style" of the so-called "silver-fork" or fashionable novel. This type of novel gave at least the illusion of depicting realistically the life and manners of English high society in the years following the end of the Napoleonic wars, a period in which the wealthy classes underwent a tremendous increase in size at the same time that the number of readers in the middle class, who—quite understandably—wanted to share vicariously the experiences of their social betters, also grew enormously: "Social etiquette at the ball, the dinner, the hunt, the club, and the opera; conversation which seldom extended beyond the shallow conventionalities of polite discourse; and a zealous attention to the details of food and clothing supplied the material for hundreds of novels by dozens of novelists." [27]

The two masterpieces of the fashionable novel were undoubtedly Disraeli's *Vivian Grey* (1826–27) and Bulwer-Lytton's *Pelham, or The Adventures of a Gentleman* (1828), each of which traces the successes of a brilliant, ambitious young man in society and politics; but there were many other such novels, particularly in the late 1820s and in the 1830s. One of the most prolific authors of such fiction was Mrs. Catherine Gore, beginning with *Women as They Are, or Manners of the Day* (1830) and *The Hamiltons, or Official Life in 1830* (1831). One of Thackeray's favorite targets for parody, Mrs. Gore almost certainly wrote *Modern Chivalry* (1843), a fashionable novel which appeared in *Ainsworth's Magazine* and which has sometimes been attributed to Ainsworth himself, though it bears no distinctive mark whatever of his authorship. Among the other better-known producers of silver-fork novels were Theodore Hook, Robert Plumer Ward, Thomas Henry Lister, the Earl of Mulgrave, Lady Charlotte Bury, Marianne Spencer-Stanhope, Charles White, and the Countess of Blessington.

Ainsworth's direct connection with this school of fiction was, at best, tenuous. If he was ever anything of a novelist of fashionable life, it was not until quite late in his career when both the silver-fork tradition and Ainsworth's own creative gifts were thoroughly diluted and when he turned increasingly from historical to contemporary subjects. The tradition seems worth mentioning here, however, because, in a roundabout way, the fact that it had flourished for a decade before the publication of *Rookwood* may help to account for the popularity of that very different, quite down-to-earth, and distinctly unfashionable novel and its successors from Ainsworth's pen:

Here was a vivid contrast of sensations which proved irresistible to the reading public, long since heartily sick of the dreary stream, which had deluged the country for the past ten years, of "Tales of Fashionable Life," wherein inane heroes named Mortimer or Mordaunt, in the intervals they could spare from Crockford's [a favorite resort of London dandies], made vapid love to the Lady Julia De Vere or her French maid; wherein "scenes" at the opera and race-course formed the incidents, the tittle-tattle of the servants' hall provided "conversation," and the amours of ballet dancers and milliners supplied the necessary spice to ensure a sale. [28]

If this explanation by S. M. Ellis is to be credited, and there seems no reason not to do so, Ainsworth's meteoric success during the 1830s may be attributed not only to his use of still highly viable historical and Gothic materials but also to his reaction against the expiring silver-fork school.

VII *Literary Influences: Nineteenth-century Melodrama*

It is dangerous to assume that a writer of fiction is influenced only by the work of other novelists. The forces that mold his art crowd in on him from all directions and are by no means limited to literature in print. In our own day, many novelists—most notably, perhaps, those associated with the "new novel" in France—owe to the film much of their technique, their notion of what constitutes reality and how it is to be depicted. Some of them, like Alain Robbe-Grillet, have worked and are thoroughly at home in both media. A nineteenth-century ancestor of the film, as pervasive in Ainsworth's time as the movies are in ours, was melodrama—"the most popular dramatic form of its age."[29] From the early years of the century on, countless scores of such plays were performed before huge audiences drawn from every segment of English society; and such mass exposure must have affected the literary sensibilities of both writers and readers in a very profound way.

Though there were several main kinds of melodrama, and though this kind of play underwent considerable modification and sophistication as the century wore on, certain common features may nevertheless be discerned in most examples of the genre. Fundamental to it was a basic conflict between virtue and vice, the noble hero and the pure heroine pitted against the deep-dyed villain. Great suspense was created when the hero or the heroine or both were placed in dire peril, but justice was inevitably served when they were providentially rescued, usually just in "the nick of time." Characters in melodrama tended to be shallow and stereotyped, and far more emphasis was placed on the depiction of action—the more sensational, the better—than on the sensitive exploration of human psychology. Partly because many of the theaters in which melodrama was acted—not only such "legitimate" houses as Covent Garden and Drury Lane but some "minor" theaters as well—were very large, subtle nuances in performance were out of the question: to be clearly heard and seen by most of the spectators, speeches had to be shouted and gestures had to be exaggerated. Innovations in stagecraft and lighting made possible ambitious scenic effects and tempted playwrights into using elaborate spectacle. "Attempted seductions, wrongful accusations, disloyalties, hidden secrets, lost parentage"[30]—certain stock themes kept recurring and they were always treated at a high pitch of emotion.

Throughout the century, the connection between the melodrama and the novel was very close. Best sellers by Scott, Ainsworth, and Dickens were frequently adapted for the stage. Later, two novels by women writers formed the bases of some of the most successful Victorian melodramas: several dramatic recastings of Mrs. Henry Wood's *East Lynne* (1861) and C. H. Hazlewood's version (1877) of Mary Elizabeth Braddon's *Lady Audley's Secret* (1862). Novelists in their turn borrowed freely many of the devices of the melodramatic playwright; and Dickens—always passionately fond of the theater—was perhaps the prime example: his novels are full of boldly drawn confrontations between good and evil, and his fondness for dwelling on injured innocence has done him considerable harm with tough-minded twentieth-century readers.

Literally from the start of Ainsworth's career as a writer, he was much drawn to the melodrama; and melodramatic devices, as we shall see in Chapter 6, persisted in his fiction to the very end. The earliest of his work to survive in print is *Ghiotto; or, Treason Discovered,* one of the plays he wrote at the age of fifteen and staged in his basement theater in King Street. Both the story and its treatment are melodrama pure and simple—melodrama of a high-flown, Gothic kind. The villainous Ghiotto, jealous of his cousin Manfred, plots to have him banished from the court of the king of Spain and assassinated along with Isabinda, who rejected Ghiotto for Manfred. The plot miscarries: one of the hired assassins stabs the other, believing him to be Manfred; and the second assassin, before he dies, reveals Ghiotto's evil scheme to the king. Short as it is, *Ghiotto* contains a number of sensational incidents.[31] As Orsino, the first assassin, prepares to swear that he is innocent, a bolt of lightning strikes him dead. When Ghiotto denies the charge of Hugo, the second assassin, that Ghiotto hired him, saying, "By the blue heaven he lied!," the lights go out. Ghiotto is challenged by Manfred:

> Approach cold Hugo's body, place thy hand
> Upon his breast, then take thy God to witness,
> That thou art innocent of this dire charge.

Reluctantly Ghiotto assents. As he touches the dead body, blood begins to flow from Hugo's wound; and the corpse opens its eyes and stares at him. Brought to bay at last, Ghiotto stabs himself. His dying words to Manfred are delivered fortissimo:

> This legacy I leave thee—Hate! hate! hate!
> May curses everlasting be thy meed!
> But, ha! hell drops me down! I come! Oh! Oh!
> (*dies*)

The gap between the mood of *Ghiotto* and that of *Rookwood,* published thirteen years later, is not a very wide one.

Just as the historical novel, the Gothic novel, the rogue novel, and the silver-fork novel inspired numerous parodies, so did the melodrama, even at the height of its popularity. In fact, the first of Ainsworth's known publications, *The Rivals: a Serio-Comic Tragedy* (written after *Ghiotto* but published in Arliss's *Pocket Magazine* a few months earlier in 1821[32]), is such a parody. This playlet (it is only three pages long) deals with the rivalry between Janvan, King of Bedoea, and Stephens Antesblan, his prime minister, for the affections of Billingtonina, a charming fishmonger. The principals rant at each other in doggerel declamation sprinkled with a dash of slang. A sample passage runs like this:

STEPHENS.
Usurper off! what are you doing there!

JANVAN.
Traitor begone! what shall Bedoea's prince
Yield aught to thee, or in his project wince?
Quickly begone, or in a porter vat
Drowned shalt thou be, I swear it, and that's flat.

STEPHENS.
Tyrant unjust I scorn thy threats and thee,
And that I'll have this maid thou soon shalt see.
Now if thou stirrest but to give command,
By Heaven, thou diest by this powerful hand.
>   [*draws*]

JANVAN. (*laughs*)
And dost thou think my sword's less sharp than thine?
Its edge less cutting and its point less fine?
Behold it now (*draws*) and if thou dar'st to fight,
Thus feel my valour and approve my might.
>   *They fight.*

The rivals kill each other; Billingtonina, in her grief, downs a glass of poisoned gin and expires also.

Unfortunately, the adolescent Ainsworth's ability to poke fun at melodramatic excesses in dialogue and situation did not persist into maturity. In his best-known work, he takes melodrama very seriously indeed, for it constitutes an essential component particularly of his historical fiction. If we are to respond favorably to these novels, therefore, we must be willing to accept their melodrama along with their other, probably more palatable, features.

In some of Ainsworth's later novels, however, though the melodramatic element does not by any means diminish, we do occasionally infer that he was somewhat uneasy about what he was doing. In *Old Court* (1867), for example, there is a passionate scene between the hero and the heroine which is clearly meant to be deeply moving. Overheard by his beautiful cousin Lucetta, young Clarence Chetwynd has just renounced all claim to her property. She rushes into the room, "her bright eyes glittering with tears," throws her arms around him, and kisses him. Lucetta thanks Clarence profusely, but insists that "I cannot allow you to give way thus to your generous impulses. I cannot—will not—accept all the property from you." Clarence, in his turn, protests that

"I will accept no part of the property. It is not mine by right, and I should hold myself in contempt if I could deprive you of any portion of it. . . . Little did I dream, when I first gazed upon your picture, that I should be able to say to you, as I do now, 'Be mistress of this old mansion, Lucetta—be mistress of those lordly domains—be mistress of all that your father would have bestowed upon me—and may you long, long, enjoy them—blest with every happiness!'"

A jarring note, but for the twentieth-century reader a very refreshing one, is sounded when Lucetta's aunt, Lady Danvers, makes her comment, through her tears, on this touching confrontation: "I declare this is quite a sentimental drama . . . and quite worth coming from Brighton to witness" (III, xiii).

In Ainsworth's next novel, *Myddleton Pomfret* (1868), there is a similar mixture of modes, a flash of melodrama and then a pulling back. The villainous Scrope Musgrave has married Sophy Curzon, who believes herself to be a widow, though her husband is actually alive under another name and Musgrave knows it. When Musgrave ultimately tells Sophy the truth, he makes it very clear, with great relish, that he had married her to avenge himself on her first husband, an old enemy. Sophy's reaction is straight from Victorian melodrama:

"You have acted infamously, Scrope. You have led me into the commission of a sin which can only be expiated by a life's penitence. My own wretchedness is increased by the thought of the hopeless misery into which your vindictive cruelty has plunged a noble-hearted man. Better have killed him than inflict such pain. Had I been the only sufferer my anguish would have been more tolerable, but it is heightened by the knowledge of his suffering. Your plan has succeeded. The evil agents you have summoned have served you well. But your triumph will be short-lived. The ill you have done will recoil on your own head. Be sure that a terrible retribution awaits you."

Instead of rejoining in kind, however, Musgrave all but tells Sophy to stop her foolish histrionics. "Bah! I laugh at such talk! . . . It may tell upon the stage, but it won't do in private life" (II, iv).

Having, in this initial chapter, attempted to explain Ainsworth's work in terms of his biography and the literary traditions to which he fell heir, we must turn now to our major task: the examination of its most prominent features. These characteristics are five in number, and to each a chapter is devoted: (1) Ainsworth's craftsmanship, the way he put his novels together, its virtues and its faults; (2) his use of historical materials; (3) the place of sensationalism in his fiction; (4) his typical characters and modes of characterization; and (5) the distinctive authorial voices which resound throughout his work.

CHAPTER 2

The Skillful Architect: Ainsworth's Plots

Romance, if I am not mistaken, is destined shortly to undergo an important change. Modified by the German and French writers—by Hoffman, Tieck, Victor Hugo, Alexandre Dumas, Balzac, and Paul Lacroix—the structure commenced in our own land by Horace Walpole, Monk Lewis, Mrs. Radcliffe, and Maturin, but left imperfect and inharmonious, requires, now that the rubbish which choked up its approach is removed, only the hand of the skilful architect to its entire renovation and perfection. (*Rookwood*, 1849 Preface)

I *General Characteristics*

LITTLE specific information about Ainsworth's working methods has survived, but we know, on the evidence of his letters to his antiquarian friend James Crossley and others, that he engaged in careful research, wherever possible in primary documents, while preparing the historical background of his novels. We know, from their appearance in serial versions already divided into books or segments otherwise labeled, that he planned them in advance at least to the extent of deciding into what major parts each of his plots should fall. Nevertheless, there is good reason to believe that Ainsworth did not meticulously work out all the details, or even the most important ones, of his narratives before starting to write. His plots, especially in the later novels, are full of inconsistencies and irrelevances. Individual characters and whole lines of action may drop out of sight, never to appear again. Digressions occur frequently. Sometimes it is difficult to be sure what or whom a given novel is about.

In regarding *The Flitch of Bacon* (1854), for example, we cannot be certain whether we are concerned primarily with a pastoral novel in which two rustic couples vie for a legendary token of marital fidelity and happiness, or with the Gothic story of Sir Walter Fitzwalter and his grim life at the gloomy, haunted house which becomes the inn of the

Dunmow Flitch. The action involving the spirited Bab Bassingbourne and the foppish Sir Gilbert de Montfichet does not fit in comfortably with either of the largely unrelated main strands of the novel. To take another problem case, it is hard to tell who the protagonist of *The Leaguer of Lathom* (1876) is. Is it the Earl of Derby, martyred for his allegiance to King Charles I during the English Civil War? Is it his heroic Countess, who bravely defends Lathom House against the siege conducted by the parliamentary forces? Or is it the gallant young Captain Frank Standish, of whose prowess we see many examples?

In some of Ainsworth's other historical novels—*Talbot Harland* (1871) and *Beatrice Tyldesley* (1878), for example—neither the fictional nor the historical characters and incidents successfully carry the weight of the plot: the fictional characters and incidents are not interesting enough, and the historical characters and incidents are not fully and consistently developed. A few of Ainsworth's titles arouse false expectations in the first-time reader and make it difficult for him to see the main thrust of those novels. When they have a power of their own, as the misnamed *The Constable of the Tower* (1861) and *Cardinal Pole* (1863) do, this factor does not matter; but the unity and the impact of a feeble novel like *Chetwynd Calverley* (1876) are not aided by the fact that its supposed protagonist is a cipher who disappears for long stretches from the center of the action.

When we bear in mind the pressures under which Ainsworth wrote, his occasional shortcomings as a craftsman do not appear surprising. What is surprising, on the contrary, is that he succeeded as often as he did in fashioning unified and effective plots. He did, after all, turn out novels with astonishing speed: usually for serial publication, with all its attendant pressures; and frequently he was writing away on more than one novel at a time. Moreover, Ainsworth, not a man to shrink from difficulties, chose to work with singularly complex materials requiring the sort of dexterity and control which no author is capable of sustaining without interruption.

A brief examination of four typical Ainsworth plots indicates some common features and some common problems.

II *Four Typical Plots*

The main plot of *Windsor Castle* (1843) is concerned with Henry VIII's attempts to divorce Catherine of Arragon* in order to be free to

* Ainsworth's spelling.

marry Anne Boleyn. Cardinal Wolsey uses a variety of devices to delay Henry's action, such as arousing his jealousy of the fickle Anne and his interest in the beautiful Mabel Lyndwood (supposedly the grand-daughter of the forester Tristram Lyndwood but actually Wolsey's natural daughter). Wolsey also arranges to have Catherine confront Henry with evidence of Anne's love for Sir Thomas Wyat. By the end of the fourth book, these stratagems of Wolsey's have failed: Henry has surrendered to the wiles of Anne, who has been aided by the Duke of Suffolk; and Wolsey is disgraced. But, in the sixth book, we see that Catherine's prophecy to Anne is borne out: just as Catherine had been rejected for Anne, so now Anne is thrown over for Jane Seymour. Henry is getting tired of Anne; and, on receiving evidence of her love for Sir Henry Norris, he has her sentenced to death and beheaded.

Windsor Castle also contains subplots involving some of Henry's courtiers. The Earl of Surrey is in love with Lady Elizabeth FitzGerald (the "fair Geraldine"); his suit is hopeless because the king opposes the match. For a time, Surrey's rival in love is the Duke of Richmond, Henry's natural son. Surrey's friend Sir Thomas Wyat incurs the king's wrath because of his ill-concealed love for Anne Boleyn; eventually, Wyat and Mabel Lyndwood fall in love.

Hovering over the whole plot of *Windsor Castle* is the devilish Herne the Hunter, who haunts Windsor Forest with his mysterious band. He becomes involved in the action at every turn, aiding mortals in their unwholesome designs in order to capture their souls. Henry time and again tries to defeat Herne, as do Surrey and Richmond, but always without success.

The Introduction of *The Lancashire Witches* (1849) also takes place in the reign of Henry VIII, but the main action is set in the next century, when the curse delivered in 1537 by John Paslew, the last abbot of Whalley, against the infant daughter of his antagonist Nicholas Demdike works itself out. Mother Demdike is one of two notorious witches infesting a region of Lancashire; her daugher Elizabeth Device and Elizabeth's children, Jem and Jennet, follow in her evil footsteps. Alizon Device, who is supposed to be Elizabeth's daughter, is, by contrast, sweet and pure; but she is actually the daughter of Alice Nutter, another witch. Alizon falls in love with Richard Assheton, scion of the chief family in the area, who returns her love. But the love and lives of the young couple are blighted by Mother Demdike's archrival, Mother Chattox. With the aid of Richard's cousin Nicholas Assheton and the ghost of Abbot Paslew (garbed as a Cistercian monk) the two chief witches, Mother Demdike and Mother Chattox, are finally burned to death; but not before they have worked a great deal of mischief. Both Richard and Alizon also die—Richard, as a result of the malevolence of Jennet; Alizon, in attempting to save her penitent mother from again falling into the Devil's power—and so does Alice Nutter, having abjured her evil ways. James I, who is regarded, because of his *Demonology,* as a great authority on witches, appears in the novel; and a great deal of Ainsworth's material is based on historical accounts of seventeenth-century witch hunts in Lancashire.

The plot of the third novel, which is set in 1744, is no less intricate. In *The Miser's Daughter* (1842), Randulph Crew, a young man newly arrived in London from Cheshire, falls in love with Hilda, daughter of Scarve the miser, an old friend of Randulph's mother. The match is opposed by Scarve, who intends Hilda for his hypocritical nephew Philip Frewin. Scarve holds Randulph in contempt because he was honorable enough to relinquish his late father's estate to the elder Crew's creditors. Randulph's rather sober-sided London uncle, Abel Beechcroft, also objects to his nephew's suit of Scarve's daughter; for Abel has hated Scarve ever since Scarve had stolen his sweetheart and had married her. Abel's younger brother, Trussell Beechcroft, introduces Randulph to the fashionable London world of Lady Brabazon, Sir Singleton Spinke, Beau Villiers, the actress Kitty Conway, and other beaux and beauties, and to such eighteenth-century haunts as the Folly on the Thames, Marylebone Gardens, Ranelagh, and Vauxhall. Randulph is also exposed to some rather irrelevant Jacobite plotting through his association with Cordwell Firebras. With the aid of the rascally attorney Diggs, Philip Frewin persuades Scarve to leave him his money; but, when Philip is killed in a duel by Randulph, the money reverts after Scarve's death to Randulph, and the young lovers can be married. There is an elaborate subplot dealing with amorous and other adventurous exploits of characters from the lower orders.

The final example is *Mervyn Clitheroe* (1858), a novel that concerns the growth of the title character to young manhood: his struggle to win the hand of Apphia, sister of his school friend John Brideoake, over the opposition of her mother, and to come into the rightful inheritance of his uncle John Mobberley's property, despite the scheming of his rival Malpas Sale and Malpas's allies, the gypsies Phaleg and Obed and the barber-surgeon Simon Pownall. Mervyn's mother is dead and his father, remarried, is in the army in India. The boy is brought up by his mother's relative, Mrs. Mervyn in Cottonborough (Manchester), where he attends the Free Grammar School. He pays frequent visits to his great-uncle and great-aunt Mobberley at their country place, Nethercrofts, in nearby Marston, where he is thrown into contact with Malpas Sale, who is also Mobberley's grandnephew. Because Mervyn gets involved in some youthful scrapes, he is stricken from Mobberley's will, though Mobberley later changes his mind and makes out a new one in Mervyn's favor. This one is stolen by Pownall; and, when Mobberley dies, Malpas appears to be heir to his property. Throughout the novel, Pownall and the gypsies use the existence of the new will to threaten Malpas and to bribe Mervyn.

While Mervyn is traveling on the Continent, Malpas worms his way into the favor of Mrs. Mervyn and Mrs. Brideoake, so that, when Mervyn returns to Cottonborough after some accidental delays have prolonged his absence, he is denied admission to his patroness's house and forbidden to see her or Apphia.

After many disappointments, Mervyn recovers the will from Pownall, with the assistance, witting or unwitting, of several quite diverse characters: Doctor Foam, the Cottonborough physician; Old Hazilrigge, the superstitious owner of Owlarton Grange; Ned Culcheth, the gamekeeper whose wife Pownall has kidnapped for Malpas; Rue, Phaleg's daughter, whom Malpas has seduced; Cuthbert Spring, a man-about-Cottonborough, in love with Hazilrigge's sister; and "Major Atherton," who turns out to be Mervyn's father. Malpas is killed in a steeplechase accident. The Brideoakes are revealed to be Jacobite nobility. Mrs. Brideoake's feelings toward Mervyn are softened by these developments and disclosures, and the novel ends with the lovers happily paired off: not only does Mervyn marry Apphia, but John Brideoake marries Hazilrigge's niece and Cuthberg Spring Hazilrigge's sister.

III *Some Common Features*

The plots of these four novels—one historical (*Windsor Castle*), one Gothic (*The Lancashire Witches*), one with a distinct period flavor (*The Miser's Daughter*), and one contemporary and semi-autobiographical (*Mervyn Clitheroe*)—resemble not only one another but also the bulk of Ainsworth's fiction in a variety of significant ways. Each involves a complicated series of more or less interrelated actions and intrigues. Each relies heavily on supernatural events or what appear to be fated occurrences. Each is interlaced with historical matter, introducing a complex dimension all its own, as well as with important architectural and scenic backgrounds. Two other features which require more extended consideration are Ainsworth's use of subplots and his fondness for legal snarls, commonly involving lost or usurped inheritances.

It must not be assumed that Ainsworth's subplots are always mere padding, loading down still further an already creaking plot. Frequently, such a subplot significantly enlarges the scope of the principal action of a novel. The main love interest in *Ovingdean Grange* (1860), for example, concerns young Clavering Maunsel, the young pride of a staunchly royalist family, and Dulcia Beard, daughter of the displaced minister of the Ovingdean parish church. Chief among the difficulties faced by the young lovers is the unsettled state of England in 1651, at the height of the Civil War, and the fact that Clavering is a fugitive from Puritan justice. In the subplot, the same kind of relationship, beset by the same obstacles, exists between Ninian Saxby, a loyal young retainer of the Maunsels, and Patty Whinchat, a maid at Ovingdean Grange. Social and political turmoil, we infer, afflicts people of all classes at this deeply troubled period.

The subplot in *Old Saint Paul's* (1841) serves to introduce a comic note into one of Ainsworth's grimmest novels. In the main action, Leonard Holt, apprentice to the grocer Stephen Bloundel, loves his master's daughter Amabel and ultimately loses her to the Earl of Rochester and the plague, but, before his loss, he undergoes incredible hardships during the great epidemic of 1665 and the London fire of the following year. Meanwhile, in the subplot, Bloundel's hypochondriac, cowardly porter Blaize eventually wins the grocer's tenderhearted servant Patience, after having incurred his own share of suffering. Leonard's character and motives are always lofty, and in the end Charles II confers a title on him in recognition of his heroism and ingenuity during the fire; but Blaize by contrast, for all he endures, remains mean and petty—a figure of fun to the end.

At times, of course, such a subplot serves as a commentary of sorts on the main action. If *The Miser's Daughter* may be said to deal with Randulph Crew's exposure to and partial involvement with the fashionable world of mid-eighteenth century London, the ludicrous misadventures of Crackanthorpe Cripps—the nephew of Abel Beechcroft's servant Jukes and himself the valet of a notorious beau—show us (and Randulph) a great deal about the values of the society which Randulph seems about to enter.

Another way a subplot enhances the meaning of the main action is shown in *The Spanish Match* (1865), in which Charles Stuart, son of James I, goes to Madrid to win the hand of the Infanta Maria. Though he fails in his suit, his attendant Richard Graham does succeed in his wooing of a Spanish maiden, thereby helping to demonstrate that the differences of nationality and religion which exist in both relationships are not enough by themselves to keep lovers apart and that peculiar circumstances, such as the machinations of Buckingham on the English side and Olivarez on the Spanish, are operating in the case of the royal pair.

Perhaps because Ainsworth was a lawyer himself, he frequently resorted to the device of basing his plots on wills, as he did in *The Miser's Daughter* and *Mervyn Clitheroe*: missing wills, stolen wills, disregarded wills, wills that have been tampered with, wills that are changed at the whim of cantankerous old men. In the world of Ainsworth's fiction, the orderly procedures of the law are capable of being subverted, usually in far-fetched but perfectly plausible ways. Individuals and societies, instead of benefiting from these procedures, suffer incredibly when they are circumvented.

For instance, Sir John Chiverton, in the very early novel which bears his name, holds Chiverton Hall in defiance of his grandfather's will by which the estate was bequeathed to Sir John's sister Ellice. The course of the whole novel depends on when this guilty secret will be revealed, to whom, and with what consequences. All the action of *Rookwood* hinges on the fact that Ranulph Rookwood is not really the heir of the late Sir Piers Rookwood, as everyone had supposed. The novel begins with the disclosure that Sir Piers was legally married to the mother of Luke, who is older than Ranulph; and this revelation sets afoot an involved series of intricate schemes and fierce rivalries. Much of Jonathan Wild's villainy in *Jack Sheppard* is explained by the fact that he has designs on the fortune of Sir Montacute Trenchard. By marrying Jack's mother, who is really Sir Montacute's daughter, and by murdering all the other possible heirs, Wild hopes to enrich himself enormously.

The *South-Sea Bubble* (1871), when it does not deal with high finance and low politics in the reigns of Queen Anne and George I, concerns itself with the fortunes of Margaret Harpledown, whose father is murdered by robbers: her preservation from the greedy clutches of her cousin Sir Blake Harpledown, who has inherited her father's money in the apparent absence of a will; and the recovery of her father's will from those who have stolen it and kept it hidden. *The Constable of the Tower*, as a final example, opens with Henry VIII at the point of death. In his will, he has named the Earl of Hertford Lord Protector (that is, virtually king during the minority of Henry's young son); but Henry begins to have misgivings about this decision and wants to make Sir

John Gage and Sir Thomas Seymour executors with powers equal to Hertford's. However, the unscrupulous Earl, with the aid of the king's physician, manages to keep Henry's advisers out of the sickroom until the original testament is ratified, in a highly suspect manner, just before the monarch's death.

IV *Two Successes*

Jack Sheppard (1839) provides a good example of Ainsworth at his best in plot construction. The novel is, as we have noted, the history of the notorious eighteenth-century robber and prison breaker, from infancy to his death by hanging at Tyburn, a span of almost twenty-two years. In recounting it, Ainsworth was faced with several problems. How does one tell such a story without turning it into a monotonous series of escapades? How does one present the criminal character in such a way as to retain some semblance of sympathy for him? How does one select the episodes to be treated, since coverage of twenty-two years is an impossibility?

Ainsworth went a long way toward solving these problems by the introduction into his narrative of two additional characters, one historical and one invented, Jonathan Wild and Thames Darrell, respectively. From the beginning, the thief and thief-catcher Jonathan Wild hovers over Jack like an evil destiny. A disappointed suitor of Jack's mother, Wild corrupts and brings to the gallows first her husband and ultimately Jack himself. Thames Darrell, Jack's foil, is his fellow apprentice in the carpenter shop of Mr. Wood of Wych Street. Like Jack, Thames is the son of a father who has died violently and of a mother who has been abused and persecuted. Also like Jack in being the object of Wild's cruelty, Thames nevertheless chooses the path of virtue and is rewarded in the end by the hand of the beautiful Winifred, his master's daughter. The stories of the two young men are closely intertwined, each lad helping us to see the other in a better, more human light; and Thames ultimately prospers through the help of Jack and Jack's lieutenant, the cutthroat Blueskin.

Ainsworth divides his plot into three "Epochs." The first and shortest, called "Jonathan Wild" and dated 1703, serves as prologue, introducing us to the twisted circumstances in which both Jack and Thames come into the world and to the evil man who is such a malevolent influence on the fortunes of both their families. Immediately after Ainsworth shows the squalor in which Mrs. Sheppard lives with her baby several months after her husband's execution, he involves his audience in the exciting chain of events during which the infant Thames Darrell is saved from his wicked uncle and is brought into the care of Mr. Wood. The action of the seven chapters which comprise this first part takes place within a few hours on the night of November 26.

The second "Epoch" is similarly concentrated, its action being packed into a few days in June, 1715; but these are very important days. Ainsworth establishes in the opening chapter a striking contrast between Wood's two apprentices, Jack ("cunning and knavery") and Thames ("frankness and honour"); and he also sketches the relationships among the inhabitants of the carpenter's house: the hapless Wood, his shrewish wife, Winifred, and the two boys. He then describes two events, both occurring on the same evening, which drastically alter the courses of Jack's and Thames's lives and which promote the main action of the novel: in a moment of anger and without justification, Mrs. Wood slaps Jack's face, and thus drives him to a life of crime under Wild's tutelage ("May I be cursed . . . if ever I try to be honest again," he says in Chapter V as he slinks away); and Thames puts himself in his uncle's power by going to his house in Southampton Fields to return a miniature of his father which Jack has stolen. As the "Epoch" ends, there is every indication that the uncle, despite his hesitation and his bitter pangs of remorse, has succeeded, again with Wild's assistance, in sending Thames to his death.

More time, six months in 1724, elapses in the third part; but Ainsworth has again set his limits with care and keeps the action moving with swiftness and coherence. At the beginning, Thames Darrell, who has not after all perished but managed to escape to France and prosper, returns to London. Immediately thereafter, Jack Sheppard, now a confirmed criminal, is shown at the height of success and in the depths of depravity, participating in the robbery of the house of his erstwhile benefactor, Mr. Wood, during which Blueskin cuts Mrs. Wood's throat. Despite everything Jack has endured at Mrs. Wood's hands, he regards this murder as an outrage and breaks with Jonathan Wild. From that point forward, Jack's efforts (between incarcerations and escapes) are directed against Wild and in behalf of Winifred, whose honor he saves, and of Thames, whom he rescues from Wild's clutches.

Jack is hanged in the end, and the interests of justice are thus served—but not before he has been reconciled with his long-suffering mother, Thames's claim to his name and fortune is assured, and Jonathan Wild's house, containing his infamous collection of ghastly relics and his stolen treasures, is burned by a mob. We are told on the penultimate page, in one of those reassuring predictions with which Ainsworth liked to close his historical narratives, that Wild himself is going to die, "seven months afterwards, with every ignominy, at the very gibbet to which he had brought his victim."

Ainsworth was equally systematic in planning another early novel, *Old Saint Paul's,* in which all the action is closely connected with the London plague year, 1665, and the great fire of 1666. There are six "Books" in the novel: each of the first five is devoted to a specific stage in the progress of the pestilence, and the sixth is given over to the fire. This division is not merely arbitrary: the rationale and the coherence of each part are clearly and persuasively worked out, and the contribution of each to the whole narrative requires no defense.

IV *Some Limited Successes*

Like *Jack Sheppard, Crichton* (1837) is divided into three sections, one short and two long; but, though Ainsworth is even more successful in *Crichton* in maintaining the swift pace which can result from observing the unity of time, he does not so effectively gather up all the threads of his plot; and the symmetry of the novel, therefore, is more apparent than real. All is well as long as our attention is concentrated on the hero, the peerless Scot James Crichton, who has come to the sixteenth-century France of Henri III to make his fortune. The first Book deals with his triumphant disputation at the Sorbonne and introduces a number of students who will play important roles in the action. Several of these young men, especially the Spaniard Caravaja, are bitterly jealous and resentful of Crichton; two befriend him: the Englishman Blunt, who is followed about everywhere by his bulldog, and Crichton's fellow Scotsman, Ogilvy. We also meet such leading characters as the helpless Gelosa, who is infatuated with Crichton, the sinister magician Ruggieri, and the masked Prince Vincenzo Gonzaga.

The action of the second Book takes place that evening, and in it the scene of Crichton's prowess is changed from the university to the intrigue-ridden court of Henri III. There, the daring Crichton rescues the Gelosa from Ruggieri's laboratory and purloins the documents which prove the identity of the princess Esclairmonde. The final Book deals with events of the following day when Crichton defends himself successfully in the lists, first against Gonzaga and then against the disguised Henri of Navarre. With Crichton's aid, the conspiracy against King Henri is revealed and foiled.

But, in this third section, Ainsworth at last seems to be overwhelmed by his complex material. To the reader's bewilderment, stratagems and counter-stratagems succeed one another with lightning rapidity. First the Gelosa and then Prince Vincenzo Gonzaga drop out of the narrative before their fates are clearly settled. Most disturbing, Crichton, who is a devout Catholic, and Esclairmonde, the Princess of Condé, who has suffered much for her Protestant faith, suddenly and unaccountably appear to overcome the religious scruples which had seemingly prevented their marriage; and, as the novel closes, the stage is set for a conventional happy ending:

"Crichton," said Esclairmonde, blushingly turning towards her lover, "have I your dispensation if I break my vow?"

"From the bottom of my heart," replied Crichton, passionately. "And I begin to find I am not so staunch a Catholic as I fancied myself when I quitted Florent Chrétien's cell."

"I would be of any creed for the woman I love," said the Bourbon.

"And I," said Henri Trois.

"Then no more need be said about the matter," said Chicot. "Let us send for a priest at once. He will remove every difficulty. Points of faith are easily settled where love plays the umpire."

That assertion is a pleasant, romantic one, but nothing in the novel prepares us for the closing line; on the contrary, "points of faith" stubbornly adhered to have been the cause of much grief during the action of *Crichton*. There are, therefore, a dishonesty and a degree of esthetic incompetence present which no amount of architectonic skill can conceal.

In *The Lancashire Witches,* too, Ainsworth succeeds during most of the novel in keeping the narrative moving swiftly forward. When interest flags somewhat toward the end, it again does so partly because content and structure have ceased to have much connection with each other. An Introduction consisting of ten chapters, set in 1536–37, provides the background and the impetus of the main body of the story, which takes place early in the seventeenth century. During the prelude, John Paslew, the last abbot of Whalley, is martyred for participating in the so-called Pilgrimage of Grace against Henry VIII. A proud and passionate man, Paslew refuses to withdraw or soften the malediction which he hurls at wizard Demdike's daughter: "Thy child shall be a witch, and the mother of witches" (ch. ix).

Indeed she will. By the time Book the First opens, three generations later, Mother Demdike has reached the zenith of her might, which is rivaled only by that of her arch-foe, Mother Chattox. It is May Day—surely the strangest May Day in all literature. The crowning of Alizon Device as Queen of the May at Whalley is ordinary enough; but, in the course of the ensuing day and night, the simple rustic revels are counterpointed by wild supernatural carryings-on, culminating in a witches' sabbath in the ruined convent church. Amid this dazzling whirl of action, the romance between Alizon and young Richard Assheton (one of whose ancestors was deeply involved in Abbot Paslew's downfall) is set moving, and Alizon learns the secret of her parentage.

The next day, which is treated in Book the Second, is hardly less crowded and exciting. The reader is given a vivid account of the power wielded by Mother Demdike and Mother Chattox; but, before this book ends, both of them die horribly. Shortly before being burned alive, Mother Demdike curses Richard and Alizon; and the reader, by now thoroughly attuned to the world of this novel, knows that their love can have no happy termination.

More than two months elapse between the end of the second Book and the beginning of the third, and this break in the onward rush of the narrative helps to account for the anticlimactic quality of the last section. Everything of consequence has really been settled by this time: Richard and Alizon are clearly doomed; and, just as clearly, Mother Demdike's progeny will be hunted down with the aid of the wrathful Abbot Paslew's ghost. Matters are not greatly helped by the introduction of James I—deus ex machina, tyrant, and buffoon—speaking in Scottish dialect and playing to the hilt his role as the "British Solomon," expert on things-in-general and witchcraft in particular. (He reappears five years later, in much the same role, in Ainsworth's *The Star-Chamber.*) The pseudo-historical material involving the king—such as his dubbing a joint of Lancashire beef "Sir-Loin"—and conversations like that in which one of his courtiers delivers a textbook comparison-and-contrast between Shakespeare and Jonson—"great as Ben Jonson is, and for wit and learning no man surpasses him, he is not to be compared with Shakespeare, who for profound knowledge of nature, and of all the highest qualities of dramatic art, is unapproachable" (ch. vii)—help to slow the narrative and to weaken action and unity.

Five other important Ainsworth novels—*Guy Fawkes, Windsor Castle, Rookwood, The Constable of the Tower,* and *The Miser's Daughter*—illustrate various ways in which even more serious organizational problems can arise despite the author's careful adherence to what looks like neat structural division. All is well during the first two of the three parts of *Guy Fawkes* (1841). These are devoted, respectively, to the evolution of the gunpowder plot of 1605 and to its betrayal; and, most skillfully managed, they convey to the reader a genuine sense of rising excitement. But in the third section, more strikingly than in the concluding part of *The Lancashire Witches*, Ainsworth rather badly lets his audience down. He devotes this section to recounting the miserable fates of the chief conspirators after the failure of the plot—of all of them, although we are really interested solely in Fawkes himself, who is given only a small share of Book the Third.

In *Windsor Castle,* even more than in *Crichton,* Ainsworth disturbs us by leaving potentially interesting loose ends untied. The structure is not really impaired by the fact that the action of Book the Sixth takes place seven years after that of the first five parts; the chief interest of the novel, after all, rests in Henry VIII's relationship with Anne Boleyn; and the sixth book, showing as it does Anne's downfall, is a logical consequence, if not an integral part, of the main action. Nor should we be disturbed by the supernatural dimension involving Herne the Hunter and his repeated incursions: these consistently affect the king and his dependents and have a definite place in advancing action and creating atmosphere. Nor, finally, does Ainsworth's penchant for dropping his role as narrator and taking up the part of architectural historian trouble particularly in *Windsor Castle*: he indulges in it to any considerable extent only in Book the Third.

What is bothersome is Ainsworth's repeated introduction of motifs which he fails to develop sufficiently. For example, the unhappy romance of Surrey and the fair Geraldine, though it serves to demonstrate Henry's power, is too sketchily treated to sustain interest. Wyat is something of an enigma: his switching his affection from Anne Boleyn to Mabel Lyndwood is not satisfactorily explained, and it is not clear how much he is in the power of Herne the Hunter. The king's pursuit of Mabel is allowed simply to stop, without explanation. Much of Book the Fifth is given over to such side issues as Herne the Hunter's lust for Mabel, the plot to blow up his stronghold, and Mabel's death while attempting to escape from his power. Despite the basic unity of the novel, then, we have the feeling that Ainsworth allows himself to stray too often from the main, broad track of his narrative and to abandon his reader at the end of little trails that lead nowhere.

These are instances of negligence: either Ainsworth did not sufficiently think through what he was doing or he temporarily forgot where he was heading. But, like other eighteenth- and nineteenth-century novelists, Ainsworth was also given to deliberate digressions which slow down the development of his plots. Such digressions, of course, are not necessarily objectionable. Only a very pedantic critic, for instance, would quarrel with Ainsworth about the fourth Book of *Rookwood* (1834), in which a closely knit, rapidly moving narrative concerning the unhappy Rookwood family is totally abandoned for an equally closely knit, rapidly moving narrative dealing with Dick Turpin's frantic ride from Kilburn to York following the accidental killing of his friend and fellow-highwayman Tom King. This episode is indeed a gripping one obviously written at white heat by Ainsworth,[1] which may be enjoyed for itself and in fact was sometimes printed separately; but it must be pointed out, however gently, that its connection with the rest of the novel is, at best, tangential.

A whole section of digressive material is involved in *Rookwood*; in other novels, countless individual chapters digress. Frequently, such digressions take the form of rather heavy-handed comic relief; at other times, Ainsworth indulges in lengthy topographical and, especially, architectural accounts. Again, some of these are quite justifiable, but a considerable number are not. For instance, in several of Ainsworth's novels dealing with the Tower, the giant warders Og, Gog, and Magog and the dwarf Xit are more often tedious than amusing. Ainsworth's more ambitious set pieces are, however, reserved for discussion in Chapters 3 and 6.

This discussion so far has dealt with novels in which Ainsworth's own division of the narrative into Books or Parts or Epochs has some significance and must be taken seriously. As we have seen in the cases of *Jack Sheppard* and *The Lancashire Witches.* Ainsworth frequently devotes the first of these sections to prefatory matter, incidents occurring years or generations before the central action of the novel. Occasionally, however, these initial parts are remote from the main body of the novel in a more disturbing way. Book I of *The Fall of Somerset* (1877), for instance, deals with Robert Ket's 1549 rebellion in Norfolk; but the connection of that episode with the real subject of *The Fall of Somerset,* the power struggle between the Dukes of Somerset and Northumberland, is quite tenuous. In a very few cases—such as that of *The Star-Chamber* (1854)—Ainsworth resorts to no division into parts, and the organization of the novel appears to suffer: it is as if the absence of an overt pattern makes it difficult for the author to keep lines of action in order. In *The Star-Chamber,* to cite just one disturbing structural feature, the prolonged intrigue involving one of King James I's courtiers Lord Roos, his mistress the Countess of

Exeter, his wronged wife, and her parents is thrust irrelevantly into the midst of action involving other principals. In still other instances, such partition into sections appears to be completely arbitrary—to be employed more from force of habit than for any valid esthetic reason.

The Miser's Daughter is a case in point. For no discernible reason, the three Books of the novel are named respectively after Randulph Crew, Trussell Beechcroft, and Abel Beechcroft. As a matter of fact, Randulph remains central throughout the novel and no great change occurs in the roles of his uncles, though the prudent Abel plays his part more noticeably in the view of the audience toward the end when the snarl of difficulties into which Randulph has got himself, partly through the influence of Trussell, must be unraveled and the narrative brought to an acceptable conclusion. Even without their titles, the three parts, as established by Ainsworth, do not represent distinct stages in the action, which flows on without a break.

In yet other Ainsworth novels, though there is plenty of action, there is no real plot—no selection and arrangement of action to fit some preconceived pattern of development. The effect of these novels, in other words, is not dependent on the artful ordering of incidents, though they do abound. Ainsworth is quite candid, for example, about his aim in *The Tower of London* (1840): "Desirous of exhibiting the Tower in its triple light of a Palace, a Prison, and a Fortress, the Author has shaped his story with reference to that end; and he has endeavoured to contrive such a series of incidents as should naturally introduce every relic of the old pile—its towers, chapels, halls, chambers, gateways, arches, and drawbridges—so that no part of it should remain unillustrated" (Preface). In a sense, then, the "protagonist" is the Tower; unlike a story which deals with a stage in the life of a human being, *The Tower of London* concerns itself with a phase in the history of a complex of buildings. If we accept this intent, we must be content to see both action and character subordinated to setting and to watch some rather extraordinary things happen to our received notions about plot.

What we have in *The Tower of London* instead of conventional plot is simply a slice of history-cum-fiction, with a definite beginning—Lady Jane Grey Dudley's arrival at the Tower as queen, July 10, 1553—and a definite end: her execution as a martyr on Tower Green, February 12, 1554. Lady Jane, however, is not the heroine of the novel, as we might suspect from this kind of symmetry: Mary Tudor really plays a larger part, and Mary's half-sister Elizabeth has a strong supporting role.

During the first, and shorter, Book of *The Tower of London*, Jane, the queen for less than a month, is supported in her unsteady claim to the throne by her ambitious father-in-law, the Duke of Northumberland, and by her husband, Lord Guildford Dudley. She is constantly—and, ultimately, successfully—plotted against by those who wish to put Mary on the throne. In the second Book, Mary is queen; and she too is the object of conspiracies, fostered chiefly by a faction which opposes her match with Philip of Spain but also by the champions of Elizabeth and the deposed Jane. When the novel ends with the beheading of Lady Jane, the effect of her death is considerably softened by the fact that she has long been doomed and has reconciled herself to her fate. Elizabeth is placed in protective custody at Woodstock and Mary is committed to a Spanish marriage which pleases no one. All that abides unimpaired, really, is "that grand relic of antiquity" (I, i), the Tower, having been the scene of one more series of turbulent events.

Just as setting dominates *The Tower of London,* so character—the character of Charles Stuart—dominates *Boscobel* (1872). The novel begins with the defeat of the Royalists at the Battle of Worcester in 1651 (Book I): most of it (Books II—VII) is taken up with an account of Charles's wanderings across the length and breadth of England as he attempts to elude capture by Cromwell's forces and to find a port where he can take passage to France. One narrow escape succeeds another, without any kind of cumulative effect; again and again we see Charles using his considerable wit and resourcefulness and demonstrating his gaiety, kindness, generosity, and (sometimes) superstition. At the conclusion of *Boscobel,* Charles receives word that a vessel has been hired for him at Shoreham, but those who have read Ainsworth's earlier novel *Ovingdean Grange,* which takes up Charles's history at this point, know that he is by no means out of danger.

With the exception of such unusual instances as *The Tower of London* and *Boscobel,* the typical Ainsworth novel is built, therefore, around a more or less well-made plot—hardly ever flawless but almost always effective: an ordered series of incidents, divided by the author into clearly defined stages and with a distinct beginning, middle, and end. One source of Ainsworth's appeal as a novelist, clearly, is his ability to tell a compelling story well; to organize it in such a way as to maintain his reader's interest; and to arouse in him, whether he is conscious of it or not, a sense that he is in the presence of a craftsman's work.

CHAPTER 3

The Good Old Times: Ainsworth's Use of History

The Good Old Times!—all times are good when old!
(*The Manchester Rebels of the Fatal '45*, VI, vii)

I *General Characteristics*

UNLIKE the greatest Victorian novelists, William Harrison Ainsworth tended to avoid writing about his own century. Only six of his forty-one novels—*Mervyn Clitheroe, Old Court, Myddleton Pomfret, Hilary St. Ives* (1870), *Chetwynd Calverley,* and *Stanley Brereton* (1881)—have contemporary settings. His preference, obviously, was to place his narratives in the past—the eras, most often, of the Tudor, Stuart, and early Hanoverian monarchs. With the exception of *Merry England* (1874) and *The Goldsmith's Wife* (1875), which take place in the fourteenth and fifteenth centuries, respectively, and *Crichton, John Law* (1864), and *The Constable de Bourbon* (1866), which are set on the Continent, it is possible to use Ainsworth's historical novels to trace the fortunes of the English crown from Henry VIII to the first three Georges, or from the early sixteenth century to the middle of the eighteenth. Unlike Scott, Ainsworth frequently thrust royalty into the center of his action, particularly in his Tudor novels: thus, Henry VIII figures largely in *Windsor Castle* and *Tower Hill* (1871), Edward VI in *The Constable of the Tower* and *The Fall of Somerset,* and Mary in *The Tower of London* and *Cardinal Pole.* (It is curious that Elizabeth, who is involved in the action of several of them as a rather peripheral character, is never depicted by Ainsworth as queen.)

An antiquarian like Scott, Ainsworth also had the narrative skill to turn the dry dust of ancient documents into the flesh and blood of living fiction; like his distinguished predecessor, too, Ainsworth understood the powerful attraction which the past—with its high drama, its pageantry, its very *past*ness—has for great numbers of readers.

We find in Ainsworth—as in Scott—a certain ambivalence about the past, and this contributes not a little to the emotional impact of his historical novels. In whatever age we live, we prize our present blessings; but it takes a very stern realist indeed to look back at former ages without at least a twinge of regret at the glory and the color which seem lacking in our own age. Thus, whereas Ainsworth speaks in *Beatrice Tyldesley* of "the famous Revolution of 1688, to which this country owes its liberty and preponderance" (IV, ii), and whereas he frequently condemns Roman Catholicism as bigotry and superstition, it is clear that part of him longs for "the good old times" before the Stuarts were exiled once and for all by the Glorious Revolution and for those even more remote ages when Roman Catholicism was the established religion of England.

Ainsworth tries, for instance, to do justice to the Catholic Mary Tudor—notorious in the popular mind as "Bloody Mary." Though Ainsworth concedes, rather lamely, that her "many good qualities . . . were overshadowed by bigotry" (a dangerous quality especially in a queen), he devotes far more space to recounting her virtues:

A portrait, perhaps too flatteringly coloured, has been left of her by Michele, but it is still nearer the truth than the darker presentations with which we are more familiar. ". . . Not only is she endowed with a spirit beyond other women who are naturally timid, but is so courageous and resolute that no adversary nor danger ever caused her to betray symptoms of pusillanimity. . . . Of her humility, piety, and observance of religious duties, it is unnecessary to speak, since they are well known, and have been proved by sufferings little short of martyrdom. . . ." A perfect mistress of Latin, French, Spanish, and Italian, she conversed in the latter language with fluency. She had extraordinary powers of eloquence when roused by any great emotion, and having a clear logical understanding, was well fitted for argument. . . . In the graceful accomplishment of the dance, she excelled, and was passionately fond of music, playing with skill on three instruments, the virginals, the regals, and the lute. She was fond of equestrian exercise, and would often indulge in the chase. She revived all the old sports and games which had been banished as savouring of mummery by the votaries of the reformed faith. One of her sins in their eyes was a fondness for rich apparel. In the previous reign, female attire was remarkable for its simplicity. She introduced costly stuffs, sumptuous dresses, and French fashions. (*The Tower of London*, II, i)

To counteract the notion that all Catholics in post-Reformation England were bloodthirsty Papist schemers, Ainsworth draws such sympathetic portraits as that of Cardinal Pole, a thoroughly good and gentle man who strives, with some success, to moderate the zeal of Mary's more fanatical advisers, or that of Sir William Radcliffe, an admirable Catholic landowner who holds in abhorrence Guy Fawkes's mad scheme to blow up Parliament and who is meant to be representative in his views of the great majority of law-abiding Catholics.

When Cavaliers are pitted against Puritans in the Civil War, Ainsworth's sympathies are clearly on the side of the former, who are depicted as loyal, gallant, and gay, whereas the parliamentary forces and their supporters tend to be humorless zealots. The difference is very clearly seen in *Boscobel* (1872) from the contrast between the highly favorable picture drawn of Charles Stuart and the highly unflattering one of Oliver Cromwell.

A similar contrast is evident in both *James the Second* (1848) and *Beatrice Tyldesley* between the last of the Stuart kings, James II, and the man who replaced James on the throne, William of Orange (later William III). James is viewed sympathetically as a good man who is capable of arousing great devotion in his supporters but who is ruined by his own vacillation and credulity, as well as by the malice and treachery of some of his key advisers. William, on the other hand, is efficient but cold; he utterly lacks the popular touch; and he is raised to power in England with the help of an unsavory collection of traitors and opportunists.

There are many other tributes in Ainsworth's novels to those Catholics and Jacobites who suffered and died for lost causes. *Preston Fight* (1875) and *The Manchester Rebels of the Fatal '45* (1873), for example, concern, respectively, the Jacobite uprisings of 1715 and 1745 in which large numbers of wealthy and successful men, Catholics and Protestant Tories alike, risked and lost all in a doomed, romantic effort to restore the Stuart dynasty.

Though the distinction is not always perfectly clearcut, it is possible for most purposes to divide historical novels such as Ainsworth's (or, for that matter, Scott's) into three general kinds. There is, first of all, that in which the center of interest lies in the actions and passions of historical figures of some prominence. Most of Ainsworth's historical novels fall into this first category: *The Tower of London, Guy Fawkes, Windsor Castle, Saint James's* (1844), *James the Second, The Constable* of the Tower, Cardinal Pole, The Spanish Match, Tower Hill, Boscobel, The Goldsmith's Wife, Merry England, Preston Fight, The Leaguer of Lathom, The Fall of Somerset, Crichton, John Law,* and *The Constable de Bourbon.*

A second kind of historical novel focuses on fictional characters but shows how they were affected by great historical events. This group includes the following novels by Ainsworth: *Old Saint Paul's, The Star-Chamber, Ovingdean Grange, Talbot Harland, The Manchester Rebels of the Fatal '45,* and *Beatrice Tyldesley.* Finally, some historical novels fail to deal in any major, significant way with either the people or the incidents that are the subject of the historian's chronicle: for all that, these novels take place in settings—physical, spiritual, social, intellectual, moral—which are distinctively characteristic of specific moments of the past. *The Lancashire Witches* belongs in this class, as do six novels with eighteenth-century settings: *Jack Sheppard, The Miser's Daughter, The Spendthrift* (1857), *The Lord Mayor of London* (1862), *The South-Sea Bubble,* and *Beau Nash* (1879).

II *Protagonists, Chiefly Historical*

Ainsworth's typical historical protagonist is trimmed to novel size by the author's dealing with one crucial phase of his life which ends in a notable success or in a clear defeat. For all the protagonist's power and distinction, and despite his agile maneuvering, he is very much a creature of the world he lives in, constantly plotted against and often thwarted. He is surrounded by adherents of various stripes—some loyal, some hypocritical; some devoted, some selfish—and these lesser figures (most of whom played roles in history not very different from those Ainsworth assigns to them, though not a few others are his inventions) do much to determine the extent of the protagonist's victory or failure. He may be monarch, nobleman, or commoner; but, whatever his station, those with any knowledge of history recall him as a romantic, colorful figure; and those whose education has been more or less deficient, like many in the mass audience of Ainsworth's day or any later age, find him brought to life more quickly and more vividly in Ainsworth's fiction than in the chronicles of all but a few highly gifted historians.

In *Windsor Castle,* Henry VIII, very much the absolute monarch, is used to having his way in all things. Nevertheless, it takes him more than three quarters of the novel to succeed in casting aside Catherine of Arragon and in giving his affair with Anne Boleyn the ratification of legal marriage. For all his authority and in spite of Anne Boleyn's cleverness, Henry confronts the powerful opposition of Catherine, who is determined to remain his queen, and of Cardinal Wolsey, who for a variety of motives is equally determined that there be no divorce. Wolsey uses a number of devices—such as stirring up Henry's jealousy of Anne and arranging for him to fall in love with Mabel Lyndwood—in his efforts to blunt or deflect the king's passion; but all are futile. Henry's craving for Anne is too strong, and she, like Catherine, is not without allies. In the last Book of the novel, as Anne herself realizes (see her exclamation "Just Heaven!" in VI, ii), a crude kind of retribution is meted out to her when Henry, having grown tired of Anne, just as he had earlier wearied of Catherine, breaks with her in order to marry Jane Seymour, just as he had once broken with Catherine in order to marry Anne.

From the beginning of the novel to the end, of course, Henry is indubitably dominant. Ruled by his passions and not by the will of others, Henry at worst suffers only delay in the gratification of his desires. In this respect, he differs markedly from most of Ainsworth's other historical protagonists, who tend, far more than he, to be at the mercy of forces which they cannot control. Two extreme cases are the king in *James the Second* and his daughter Queen Anne in *Saint James's*; even more than her father, Anne is the hapless plaything of her advisers—first the Duchess of Marlborough and then Abigail Hill (and, through Abigail, Robert Harley).

More typically, Henry VIII's brother-in-law Thomas Seymour—later Baron Seymour of Sudley and Lord High Admiral of England—is clearly the center of interest in *The Constable of the Tower*. Despite his very appreciable assets, he is constantly opposed and ultimately foiled in his bid for greater power. That his elder brother, Edward Seymour, Earl of Hertford (and later Duke of Somerset), and not he, has been made Lord Protector during the minority of Edward VI rankles in the mind of the ambitious Thomas Seymour. In every way possible, he tries to strengthen his position: he woos both Princess Elizabeth and Henry VIII's widow, Catherine Parr, finally marrying the latter without abandoning his designs on the former; he enriches himself by a variety of illegal schemes in order to pay off the numerous adherents whom he hopes to win over to his plan for overthrowing his brother; but, on the verge of accomplishing his aims, he is betrayed by his follower Ugo Harrington and is executed. All his cleverness and daring do not suffice against the powerful adversaries whom he takes on.

More often than not, Ainsworth's historical protagonists are in Thomas Seymour's position rather than in Henry's: the fugitive Charles Stuart, hounded all over England by Cromwell's forces; Guy Fawkes, engaged, against incredible odds, in a desperate plot which seems doomed from the start; even Jack Sheppard, who defies not only the constituted establishment of law and order but also the criminal hierarchy of Jonathan Wild. By putting such protagonists in disadvantageous positions of limited power, Ainsworth adds suspense to his narratives and heightens sympathy in his readers: who, after all, can have much fellow-feeling for an invincible Crichton, and what doubt is there that all will come right with him?

Though Ainsworth ranged freely among the great and the notorious of English history in selecting the protagonists of his fiction, it is by no means true that the center of attention in these books always rests in such figures. Some of Ainsworth's most effective historical novels are concerned primarily with characters of his own creation, and the famous names of the English past are kept in the background.

In *Old Saint Paul's,* for instance, the human interest clearly lodges in Leonard Holt, the Bloundels, and Nizza Macascree, the mysterious girl Leonard eventually marries. The Earl of Rochester does, to be sure, play a considerable role; but it is subordinate to the parts of the characters just mentioned; and though Charles II does make an appearance toward the end, he is pretty much limited to the position of a deus ex machina. What *is* true about *Old Saint Paul's*, and what establishes its position as a genuine historical novel, is that its action could not have taken place in the same way at any other period than the one depicted, from April, 1665 to September, 1666. Not only are the plague and the great London fire inescapable in their bearings on all the principals: the social, political, and economic realities of England during the Restoration are closely connected with such developments as Amabel's succumbing to Rochester, the discovery of the noble background of the so-called Nizza Macascree, Leonard Holt's rise from apprentice to partner in Stephen Bloundel's business, and the king's conferring a title on Leonard.

In *Ovingdean Grange*, again, a number of historical personages, most notably Charles Stuart, appear; but our interest, for more than half the novel at any rate, is chiefly devoted to the fictitious Maunsel family, especially Clavering Maunsel, and to Clavering's love for Dulcia Beard. The historical background is essential to the novel, for only at the time of the Civil War could the Maunsels and the Beards have found themselves in the uncomfortable position they occupy in *Ovingdean Grange,* but we tend to care about the plight of the fugitive Charles only in so far as it affects the fortunes of the principal characters. Perhaps the most important thing Charles Stuart does in the novel is to intervene with Colonel Maunsel in behalf of Clavering and Dulcia, thereby overcoming the old Cavalier's objections to the marriage of his son to the daughter of so lowly a man as the Reverend Ardingly Beard.

The action of *Ovingdean Grange,* then, is the consequence of the great events of 1651, just as that of *Old Saint Paul's* depends on the ravages which London was suffering in 1665 and 1666. In another kind of historical novel, however, the connection between fiction and fact is less precise: what matters is the general period in which the novel is set. Only in the reign of James I (whose own part in the novel, as I indicated earlier, is largely mechanical) was witchcraft viewed in precisely the way it is regarded in *The Lancashire Witches,* though Ainsworth seriously compromises his own position by entering whole-heartedly into the spirit of the age about which he is writing. Not content simply to report its superstitions and the stern measures people then took against those whom they supposed to be witches, he seems to accept the existence of incredible supernatural beings, thus going well beyond what one expects from a historical novelist in the way of sympathy with the period whose manners and morals he records.

Only in the middle of the eighteenth century would Randulph Crew have found the kind of capital which he enters in *The Miser's Daughter.* The London pleasure haunts of the day, in each of which important action takes place, are carefully described by Ainsworth; and the fashionable beaux and ladies, as well as the distinctly unfashionable Jacobite plotters, who prance and skulk through the pages of the novel are decidedly creatures of their era. The virtues of this novel are clearly recognized when it is contrasted with a much feebler late novel set at almost exactly the same period, *Beau Nash,* in which mid-eighteenth-century Bath—for all Ainsworth's considerable efforts—has none of the vivid ambience we sense in the mid-eighteenth-century London of *The Miser's Daughter.*

III *Historical Backgrounds*

But even *The Miser's Daughter* is something of a period piece, in which appropriate backgrounds are deliberately worked in so as to give a flavor of authenticity to the proceedings. Ainsworth's use of settings in some of his most famous historical novels was considerably more vital. One way in which he succeeded in making the past come alive was, as we have seen, to build certain of his books around important architectural monuments, such as the Tower of London, the original St. Paul's Cathedral, or Windsor Castle. These structures became more than mere two-dimensional backdrops: they were so thoroughly integrated with the other materials of the novels that—as we have already observed in the case of *The Tower of London*—they took on the stature of vital participants in the action. Ainsworth's use of these buildings also served another purpose: they helped to provide unity by acting as foci around which everything else in the novels could be organized.

Old Saint Paul's, for instance, is aptly named. We see the "venerable and majestic fabric" for the first time in the second chapter, as Leonard Holt hurries past it on his way to fetch a doctor to attend his master's plague-stricken son; and we return to it again and again throughout the novel, seeing it in a variety of roles: as a favorite rendezvous; as a sanctuary for the rascally Chowles and his accomplice, the ghoulish plague nurse Judith Malmayns, and a hiding place for their ill-gotten loot; as a hospital during the plague; as a center of activity during the great fire, which ultimately consumes it. Many of the most memorable scenes are enacted there: in a novel replete with the horrific, few descriptions are as chilling as the picture Ainsworth draws of the cathedral while it is being used as a pest-house; among the many exciting incidents, few can vie with the incineration of the prophetic religious enthusiast Solomon Eagle on its battlements or with the ghastly death of Chowles and Judith, who are trapped in the vaults beneath St. Paul's between roaring flames and a relentless stream of molten lead.

Ainsworth was not always able to resist the temptation to assume, from time to time, the part of antiquarian rather than storyteller; but, more often, he does not allow the narrative to flag while he recounts architectural history. In *The Tower of London*, he spaces his descriptions judiciously throughout the novel in such a way as to heighten the effect of the novel rather than detract from it. To cite but one of many possible examples, Lady Jane is informed that she is to be imprisoned in the Brick Tower. We hear no more about "the structure destined for her reception" until she is acutally led into it:

This, as has already been intimated, was the Brick Tower, the next turret on the east of the Bowyer Tower. The upper story, which is of brick—whence its name—was erected in the reign of Edward the Fourth, or Richard the Third: the basement story is of stone, and of much greater antiquity.

Entering a narrow passage, she was ushered by the officer into a small room, which he informed her was prepared for her reception. Everything that circumstances would admit appeared to have been done to lessen the rigour of her confinement. The stone walls were hung with arras; and much of the furniture—a carved oak table, and velvet-covered seats, placed in the deep embrasures of the windows—had been brought from Jane's late chamber in the palace.

"This seat," said the officer, pointing to a curiously-carved chair, "was used by Queen Anne Boleyn during her imprisonment. I had it brought hither for your ladyship's accommodation."

"I thank you for your consideration, sir," replied Jane; "it will serve to support one as unhappy as that ill-fated princess."

Having inquired whether she had any further commands with which it was possible for him to comply, and being answered in the negative, the officer took his departure, and Jane was left alone.

Alone! the thought struck chill to her heart. She was now a solitary captive. She heard the door of her prison bolted—she examined its stone walls, partly concealed by the tapestry—she glanced at its iron-barred windows, and her courage forsook her. . . . She then knelt down beside the chair, and burying her face in her clasped hands, prayed deeply and fervently for support through her trial. And she prayed not in vain. She soon afterward arose tranquil and refreshed. (II, ii)

Description and history, here and in many other places, are subordinated to action and characterization.

The most striking apparent exception to this general practice in *The Tower of London* occurs in Book II, Chapter IV, where Ainsworth devotes more than a dozen pages to an account of the Tower's history from the time of William the Conqueror down to the nineteenth century. Though decidedly a digression from the main narrative, this interruption is by no means indefensible. Late on the night of Mary's entrance into the Tower, we are shown Simon Renard, the Spanish ambassador and the real power behind the new queen, leaving a late meeting of the council at which there has been protracted discussion of sensitive matters of state. He is "fevered and wearied," and paces up and down in the palace grounds, "pondering upon recent events, and revolving future schemes within his plotting brain," when he meets a warder, who agrees to take him to the top of the White Tower.

The "glorious panorama" (II, iii) from the summit thrills the Spaniard: after all, he is gazing on the mighty city which is now virtually under his control. The warder requires little urging to tell his restless, ambitious companion the story of the Tower (which Ainsworth takes up where the warder leaves it off). It is, of course, primarily a story of cruelty and intrigue; and, when the warder, following its completion, takes Renard on a tour of the battlements, the ambassador, wearing a "sinister smile," is especially intrigued by the sight of the scaffold on Tower Hill. "There," he observed, "is the bloody sceptre by which England is ruled. From the palace to the prison is a step—from the prison to the scaffold is another." The warder's thoughts are drawn to Lady Jane, and so are Renard's, but in a different way:

"Well, if she is spared who, though placed foremost in the wrongful and ill-advised struggle, was the last to counsel it, I care not what becomes of the rest. Poor Lady Jane! Could our eyes pierce yon stone walls," he added, pointing to the Brick Tower, "I make no doubt we should discover her on her knees. She passes most of her time, I am informed, in prayer."

"Humph!" ejaculated Renard. And he half muttered, "She shall either embrace the Romish faith, or die by the hand of the executioner."

The next person Renard meets, just before the chapter ends, is Mauger, the headsman; and, when Renard expresses a desire to speak with him, the reader suspects that Lady Jane's lot is indeed desperate. Even here, then, architectural history is not merely interpolated; it has a decided part in creating mood, establishing motivation, and advancing action.

Ainsworth is not always this successful in integrating historical backgrounds into his narratives. As we shall see in greater detail in Chapter 6, he was much given to inserting lengthy set pieces of description in his novels, and even the accounts of famous old buildings which he does so well do not always come off. For example, in *The Lord Mayor of London*—a weak novel for all its entertaining features—such structures as Guildhall and the Mansion House are very elaborately described; and, since far more is made of their history than their use as settings justifies, it is difficult to resist the suspicion that—along with some quite irrelevant accounts of the political chicanery attendant on the beginnings of George III's reign—this material is included merely to pad out a rather thin and conventional plot.

As we have already noted, Ainsworth's historical sketch of the Tower in *The Tower of London* (II, iv) continues past the period dealt with in his novel until his own.

... we might relate how Thomas Howard, Duke of Norfolk, was beheaded; how the dungeons were crowded with recusants and seminary priests; amongst others, by the famous Jesuits, fathers Campion and Persons; how Lord Stourton, whose case seems to have resembled the more recent one of Lord Ferrers, was executed for the murder of the Hartgills; how Henry Percy, Earl of Northumberland, shot himself in his chamber, declaring that the jade Elizabeth should not have his estate; and how the long catalogue was closed by the death of the Earl of Essex.

How, in the reign of James the First, Sir Walter Raleigh was beheaded, and Sir Thomas Overbury poisoned. How, in that of Charles the First, Thomas Wentworth, Earl of Strafford, and Archbishop Laud, underwent a similar fate. How, in 1656, Miles Sunderland, having been condemned for high treason, poisoned himself; notwithstanding which, his body, stripped of all apparel, was dragged at the horse's tail to Tower-hill, where a hole had been digged under the scaffold, into which it was thrust, and a stake driven through it. How, in 1661, Lord Monson and Sir Henry Mildway suffered, and in the year following Sir Henry Vane. How in the same reign Blood attempted to steal the crown [an attempt Ainsworth was to deal with in his *Talbot Harland*] ; and how Algernon Percy and Lord William Russell were executed.

How, under James the Second, the rash and unfortunate Duke of Monmouth perished. How, after the rebellion of 1715, Lords Derwentwater and Kenmure were decapitated; and after that of 1745, Lords Kilmarnock, Balmerino, and Lovat. How, in 1760, Lord Ferrers was committed to the Tower for the murder of his steward, and expiated his offence at Tyburn. How Wilkes was imprisoned there for a libel in 1762; and Lord George Gordon for instigating the riots of 1780. How, to come to our own times, Sir Francis Burdett was conveyed thither in April 1810; and how, to close the list, the Cato-street conspirators, Thistlewood, Ings, and others, were confined there in 1820.

It is an imposing, even an awesome, sketch, to be sure; but it cannot really be justified in terms of its contribution to the novel, as distinct from its contribution to the reader's knowledge.

Again and again, Ainsworth views his historical backgrounds with a kind of double vision: seeing them as they were at some period in the past and contrasting them with their present, usually debased, appearance. Once more, *The Tower of London* furnishes an excellent example. Having explained some of the changes which the Tower has undergone through the centuries, Ainsworth argues that its aspect in the nineteenth century—with which a good many of his readers were no doubt well acquainted—was nothing to what it had been in days gone by:

> Viewed from the summit of the White Tower, especially on the west, the fortress still offers a striking picture. In the middle of the sixteenth century, when its outer ramparts were strongly fortified—when the gleam of corslet and pike was reflected upon the dark waters of its moat—when the inner ballium walls were entire and unbroken, and its thirteen towers reared their embattled fronts—when within each of those towers state prisoners were immured—when its draw-bridges were constantly raised, and its gates closed—when its palace still lodged a sovereign—when councils were held within its chambers—when its secret dungeons were crowded—when Tower-hill boasted a scaffold, and its soil was dyed with the richest and best blood in the land—when it numbered among its inferior officers, jailers, torturers, and an executioner—when all its terrible machinery was in readiness, and could be called into play at a moment's notice—when the steps of the Traitor's Gate were worn by the feet of those who ascended them—when, on whichever side the gazer looked, the same stern prospect was presented—the palace, the fortress, the prison—a triple conjunction of fearful significance—when each structure had dark secrets to conceal— when beneath all these ramparts, towers, and bulwarks, were subterranean passages and dungeons—*then,* indeed, it presented a striking picture both to the eye and mind. (II, iv)

Ainsworth seems constantly to be trying to remind his readers, living in an age of urbanization and industrialization in which historic old landmarks were being swept away or defaced or "restored" beyond recognition, that they had a heritage, one very largely vested in physical structures of one kind or another, and that that heritage, already gravely threatened, might soon be gone beyond recall. Such implicit warnings are by no means confined to London settings: the provincial cities and towns, too, were affected. Manchester, for instance, the city of Ainsworth's birth, had undergone vast changes since the eighteenth century. In 1724, he points out in *The Manchester Rebels of the Fatal '45,* it was still possible to refer to Manchester as a village; twenty years later it was a village no more. But it was still a far cry from the nineteenth-century Manchester which he had described in *Mervyn Clitheroe*:

> The streets had a cheerful, bustling look, denoting that plenty of business was going on, but they were not crowded either with carts or people. The country was close at hand, and pleasant fields could be reached in a few minutes' walk from the market-place.

Seen from the ancient stone bridge spanning the Irwell, the town still presented a picturesque appearance. . . . In all the narrow streets surrounding the collegiate church the houses bore the impress of antiquity, having served as dwelling-places for several generations. In Mill-gate, in Toad-lane, in Hanging Ditch, and Cateaton-street, scarcely a modern habitation could be descried. All the houses, with their carved gables, projecting upper stories, and bay-windows, dated back a couple of centuries. . . .

From this glance at Manchester in 1745, it will be seen that it formed an agreeable mixture of an old and new town. The rivers that washed its walls were clear, and abounded in fish. Above all, the atmosphere was pure and wholesome, unpolluted by the smoke of a thousand factory chimneys. In some respects, therefore, the old town was preferable to the mighty modern city. (I, ii)

Undoubtedly the most extreme example of this double vision occurs in *Auriol* (1865), Ainsworth's chaotic fantasy about a young man and a dwarf who swallow an elixir in 1600 and live on into the nineteenth century. The dwarf, known as Flapdragon or Old Parr, talks endlessly about the capital as it was under Elizabeth and how it has deteriorated with time and growth:

"I've seen this great city of London pulled down, and built up again—if that's anything. I've seen it grow, and grow, till it has reached its present size. You'll scarcely believe me, when I tell you, that I recollect this Rookery of ours—this foul vagabond neighborhood—an open country field, with hedges round it, and trees. And a lovely spot it was. Broad St. Giles's, at the time I speak of, was a little country village, consisting of a few straggling houses standing by the roadside, and there wasn't a single habitation between it and Convent-garden (for so the present market was once called); while that garden, which was fenced round with pales, like a park, extended from Saint Martin's-lane to Drury-house, a great mansion situated on the easterly side of Drury-lane, amid a grove of beautiful timber. . . . The whole aspect of the place is altered. The Thames itself is unlike the Thames of old. Its waters were once as clear and bright above London-bridge as they are now at Kew or Richmond; and its banks, from Whitefriars to Scotland-yard, were edged with gardens. And then the thousand gay wherries and gilded barges that covered its bosom—all are gone—all are gone! . . . London is a mighty city, wonderful to behold and examine, inexhaustible in its wealth and power; but in point of beauty, it is not to be compared with the city of Queen Bess's days. You should have seen the Strand then—a line of noblemen's houses—and as to Lombard-street and Gracechurch-street, with their wealthy goldsmiths' shops—but I don't like to think of 'em." (I, iii).

When Ainsworth deals with the recent past, as he does in the semi-autobiographical *Mervyn Clitheroe,* his practice is quite different. He tried, as he made clear to a number of correspondents,[1] to set down in the novel his recollections of many of the places and people he knew in childhood. Much of the book, therefore, conveys the affectionate and nostalgic tone which such reminiscence is likely to have, particularly in his account of his schooling at the Cottonborough (Manchester) Free Grammar School. He did not attempt, in this instance, to idealize the past, however: though his boyhood was by no means so grim as Dickens's, his fictional counterpart does have more than his share of troubles, and the setting in which he grows up is not at all uniformly idyllic. We find, for example, this description of Cottonborough—a far cry from "Manchester in 1745":

It was early morning, and the bustle of the day had not begun, but the pavements were thronged by troops of pale-faced men, young women, and sickly-looking children of both sexes, flocking to their unwholesome employment in the cotton-mills. The thunder of the engine announced that work had already commenced—if, indeed, it had ever ceased—in these enormous structures; and jets of gas lighting up the interior, showed the rollers, cylinders, and flying wheels of the spinning machines pursuing their course. The sight had no attractions for me, and hurrying on, I soon found myself in the country. (II, iii)

Manchester, in its early years as a center of the industrial revolution, surely seems to be the stuff of "history" in our eyes, but it is a kind of "history" with which Ainsworth was not characteristically concerned in his fiction. By the second decade of the nineteenth century, and even more by the time Ainsworth began to write novels, the mass of English readers, if not the country as a whole, had become middle class and urban. The sort of history which interested this audience was not that which was being made all around them: it was, rather, that which had taken place in the more or less remote, and always (or so it seemed) more splendid, past, when kings really ruled and heroes and rogues were painted in more glaring colors than had survived into the drab industrial present. This kind of history Ainsworth gave them, again and again, in his best novels.

CHAPTER 4

The Violent World of Harrison Ainsworth

I Suffering, Violence, and Cruelty

WITH a few exceptions, the fiction of William Harrison Ainsworth does not deal with the placid sort of domesticity which was the usual subject matter of the great mid-Victorian novelists. By and large, Ainsworth's fictional world was a singularly violent one that was marked by turmoil, cruelty, and intrigue; and this aspect is undeniably a side of his work which must appeal to certain strains of our twentieth-century sensibility. Many of us have, after all, survived the bloodiest of wars; we have become inured to the phenomena of extermination camps and genocide; for years now, we have lived on the brink of universal destruction, of a particularly horrible kind, in an atomic holocaust; and, lately, strife and disorder have come to many of our cities. Our fiction and our drama leave little to the imagination in their Naturalistic and exaggerated depiction of suffering and degradation: in this age of horrors, it is small wonder that the theater of cruelty flourishes and that the Gothic novel enjoys a revival.

As we have already had occasion to note, Ainsworth's use of history is by no means restricted to romanticizing the past. On the contrary, in dealing with its most colorful episodes he is inevitably led to accounts of passion and violence. Even a novel with such an innocent-sounding title as *Merry England* becomes a virtually unbroken account of destruction and slaughter: it is the story of the Peasants' Revolt of 1381; and, before Wat Tyler and his associates are finally put to death, the reader is exposed to scores of pages detailing instances of arson, pillage, and murder.

The interest in these novels is not solely antiquarian. There is, for example, something timely in the story of Leonard Holt, the hero of *Old Saint Paul's*, who endures in 1665 and 1666 experiences not very different in degree from those which would have been his lot had he been at Auschwitz in 1944 or at Hiroshima in 1945. He survives two attacks of the plague, and he is witness to incredible scenes of suffering and devastation. The mass grave into which victims of the London plague are thrown, for instance, vividly recalls the horrible pictures of Nazi atrocities which we have seen (and it must be admitted that Ainsworth writes of it with a certain zest):

Holding a handkerchief steeped in vinegar to his face, Leonard ventured to the brink of the pit. But even this precaution could not counteract the horrible effluvia arising from it. It was more than half filled with dead bodies; and through the putrid and heaving mass many disjointed limbs and ghastly faces could be discerned, the long hair of women and the tiny arms of children appearing on the surface. It was a horrible sight—so horrible, that it possessed a fascination peculiar to itself, and, in spite of his loathing, Leonard lingered to gaze at it. Strange and fantastic thoughts possessed him. He fancied that the legs and arms moved—that the eyes of some of the corpses opened and glared at him—and that the whole rotting mass was endowed with animation. (III, iv)

This is by no means the only graphic description of the ravages of disease and fire in *Old Saint Paul's*; indeed, the whole novel is permeated by an atmosphere of death and devastation on an epic scale, which makes the merely human concerns of the characters seem petty by comparison.

Not only impersonal forces such as those unleashed in *Old Saint Paul's* debase the quality of life in Ainsworth's novels: human beings, too, show themselves capable of unparalleled (and, frequently, un-motivated) malignity and cruelty. The character of Jonathan Wild in *Jack Sheppard* perhaps serves as an instructive example. Driven by a will to power that defies rational explanation, Wild is determined to control the criminal underworld of London and to ruin Jack Sheppard: to ruin him, moreover, in a protracted way that will be especially painful to all concerned:

"I owed his father a grudge: that I settled long ago. I owe his mother one, and will repay the debt, with interest, to her son. . . . To be complete, my vengeance must be tardy. Certain of my prey, I can afford to wait for it. Besides, revenge is sweetened by delay; and I indulge too freely in the passion to rob it of any of its zest; I've watched this lad—this Sheppard—from infancy; and, though I have apparently concerned myself but little about him, I have never lost sight of my purpose. I have suffered him to be brought up decently—honestly; because I would make his fall the greater, and deepen the wound I meant to inflict upon his mother. From this night I shall pursue a different course; from this night his ruin may be dated. . . . When I have steeped him to the lips in vice and depravity; when I have led him to the commission of every crime; when there is neither retreat nor advance for him; when he has plundered his benefactor, and broken the heart of his mother—then—but not till then, I will consign him to the fate to which I consigned his father" (II, xvi).

Wild's violent instincts turn against anyone who is in some way inconvenient to him. When, for example, Thames Darrell's wicked uncle, Sir Rowland Trenchard, from whom Wild has extracted large sums of money, ceases to be useful to him, Wild and a grimy associate unhesitatingly put him to a horrible death. As Wild pretends to get some refreshment for Trenchard, who is visiting him in his den, Mendez

darted swiftly and silently behind Sir Rowland, and flung a cloth over his head; while Jonathan, rushing upon him in front, struck him several quick and violent blows in the face with the bludgeon. The white cloth was instantly dyed with crimson; but regardless of this, Jonathan continued his murderous assault. The struggles of the wounded man were desperate—so desperate, that in his agony he overset the table, and, in the confusion, tore off the cloth, and disclosed a face horribly mutilated, and streaming with blood. So appalling was the sight, that even the murderers—familiar as they were with scenes of slaughter—looked aghast at it. (III, xii)

Gravely wounded though he is, Trenchard continues the struggle. While Mendez holds a light, Wild backs Trenchard on to the bridge over a disused indoor well:

Disengaging his right arm, Jonathan struck his victim a tremendous blow on the head with the bludgeon, that fractured his skull; and, exerting all his strength, threw him over the rails, to which he clung with the tenacity of despair.

"Spare me!" he groaned, looking upwards. "Spare me!"

Jonathan, however, instead of answering him, searched for his knife, with the intention of severing his wrist. But not finding it, he had again recourse to the bludgeon, and began beating the hand fixed on the upper rail, until by smashing the fingers, he forced it to relinquish its hold. He then stamped upon the hand on the lower banister, until that also relaxed its gripe. Sir Rowland then fell. A hollow plunge, echoed and re-echoed by the walls, marked his descent into the water. "Give me the link," cried Jonathan.

Holding down the light, he perceived that the wounded man had risen to the surface, and was trying to clamber up the slippery sides of the well.

"Shoot him! shoot him! Put him out of hish mishery," cried the Jew.

"What's the use of wasting a shot?" rejoined Jonathan, savagely. "He can't get out."

After making several ineffectual attempts to keep himself above water, Sir Rowland sank, and his groans, which had become gradually fainter and fainter, were heard no more. (III, xiii)

Both Wild's cruelty and Ainsworth's detailed account of it surpass what was usual in Victorian fiction.

Before we leave the subject of Jonathan Wild, it may be well to take another look at his house in the Old Bailey. Outside, this "large, dismal-looking habitation" has the appearance of a prison, an impression heightened inside by the grated windows, the barred doors, and the cell-like aspect of the rooms. Wild employs a sinister porter who, "with his huge bunch of keys at his girdle, his forbidding countenance and surly demeanour, seemed to be borrowed from Newgate." The house is also a museum, one which reflects the peculiar tastes of its owner. The walls of Wild's audience chamber are lined with display cases, in which a variety of "interesting objects were carefully arranged, classed, and . . . labelled":

On this side was a razor with which a son had murdered his father; the blade notched, the haft crusted with blood; on that, a bar of iron, bent, and partly broken, with which a husband had beaten out his wife's brains. As it is not, however, our intention to furnish a complete catalogue of these curiosities, we shall merely mention that in front of them lay a large and sharp knife, once the property of the public executioner, and used by him to dissever the limbs of those condemned to death for high treason; together with an immense two-pronged flesh fork, likewise employed by the same terrible functionary to plunge the quarters of his victims in the caldrons of boiling tar and oil. Every gibbet at Tyburn and Hounslow appeared to have been plundered of its charnel spoil to enrich the adjoining cabinet, so well was it stored with skulls and bones, all purporting to be the relics of highwaymen famous in their day. Halters, each of which had fulfilled its destiny, formed the attraction of the next compartment; while a fourth was occupied by an array of implements almost innumerable, and utterly indescribable. (II, xvi)

In this ghastly collection, Tom Sheppard's skull and the rope by which he was hanged are the special objects of pride to their owner.

Torture seems to exert a particular fascination for Ainsworth. His precise accounts of it, in such novels as *Jack Sheppard, Guy Fawkes,* and *The Tower of London,* go far beyond the call of duty; and the reader of these books soon becomes something of an authority on such devices as the rack, the wheel, the thumbscrew, the branding iron, the gauntlets, the pincers, the scavenger's daughter, the dungeon among the rats, and the *peine forte et dure.* Particularly unsparing is Ainsworth's description of the interrogation of Guy Fawkes: little is left to the imagination, either about the instruments employed or the agony suffered by the victim. Ainsworth, who is also fond of execution scenes, repeatedly explains in much detail the proceedings at the block, the gallows, and the stake. Again, the modern sensibility finds itself in familiar terrain.

II *The Gothic Strain*

Relevant as it may be to consider Ainsworth in terms of his effect on the twentieth-century reader, it is at least equally appropriate to regard him as a somewhat belated practitioner of a kind of fiction which flourished a generation or so before he began to write: the Gothic novel. With as much relish as any of his predecessors, Ainsworth energetically fabricates chains of sensational and shocking incidents, indulges freely in the supernatural, and shows a marked preference for such evocative settings as ancient and mysterious manor houses, abbeys, castles, or palaces—frequently ruined ones.

There is no better representative of the Gothic strain in Ainsworth's work than *Rookwood* (1834), which begins with shudders that do not often abate as the novel continues.[1] It opens as two men, an old sexton and his grandson Luke, are talking in hushed tones in "a sepulchral vault, and at midnight," while a sputtering candle throws "opaque and fantastical shadows." Seated on a coffin, surrounded by stacked coffins, they are discussing Sir Piers Rookwood, who has just died, and his clandestine relationship with Luke's late mother. The sexton has brought Luke to this place expressly to tell him that Sir Piers was her murderer, and Luke's reaction is everything the old man could have wished:

"Dead mother! upon thee I call. If in thy grave thou canst hear the cry of thy most wretched son, yearning to avenge thee—answer me if thou hast the power. Let me have some token of the truth or falsity of these wild suppositions, that I may wrestle against this demon. But no," he added, in accents of despair, "no ear listens to me, save his to whom my wretchedness is food for mockery."

"Could the dead hear thee, thy mother might do so," returned the sexton. "She lies within this space."

Luke staggered back, as if struck by a sudden shot. He spoke not, but fell with a violent shock against a pile of coffins, at which he caught for support.

One of the coffins falls to the ground, with a "thundering crash"; it splits open, and "a dead body, clothed in all the hideous apparel of the tomb," rolls out (I, i). It is, of course, Luke's mother's corpse, remarkably well preserved. Luke seizes her hand and kisses it; and, oblivious to what his companion is doing, does not relinquish his hold when the sexton attempts to replace the body in the coffin. As a result, "the hand, detached from the socket at the wrist, remained within the gripe of Luke" (I, ii). We must quickly point out that this never-to-be-forgotten opening scene does have a plot function: there is a wedding ring on the hand; Luke's mother, we learn, had been married to Sir Piers; and Luke is, therefore, his father's rightful heir. Much of the rest of *Rookwood* deals with Luke's attempt to establish his legitimacy and claim his inheritance.

Other sensational scenes abound in the novel. There is, for example, Luke's wedding, which also takes place in a subterranean vault: St. Cyprian's cell, beneath a gypsy hideout, the ruined Davenham Priory. His bride, Eleanor Mowbray, is dazed from the effects of a love potion; Luke has abandoned his gypsy sweetheart, Sybil Lovel, in order to marry her. As the wedding party approaches the altar, the light of the single torch falls on "the ghastly corpse of a female, with streaming hair, at the altar's feet." It is, of course, the body of Luke's mother. This uninvited guest is removed, and the ceremony proceeds, but not until the gypsies present have sung a wild wedding chorus and the light is inexplicably extinguished. Sybil's grandmother predicts the death of Luke's young wife; but, when light is restored, the bride, with Luke's mother's ring on her finger, is revealed to be Sybil herself.

Throughout the scene, Ainsworth has paid careful attention to its visual aspects—"a picture worthy of Rembrandt or Salvator": "those wild and fierce faces by the ruddily-flashing torchlight, which lent to each a stern and savage expression; ... those scowling visages surrounding a bride from whose pallid cheeks every vestige of colour, and almost of animation, had fled; and a bridegroom, with a countenance yet more haggard, and demeanour yet more distracted" give the spectacle the aspect of "some horrible ceremonial, practised by demons rather than human beings" (III, xi). Participants and observers alike express their powerful emotions in passionate exclamations and bursts of song; indeed, the scene—and the novel as a whole—is redolent of the atmosphere of the nineteenth-century stage.

Another memorable episode involving a corpse occurs in *The Tower of London.* The monstrous jailer Nightgall digs a grave in the vault beneath the Devilin Tower for the wasted body of a female prisoner, Alexia, whom he wishes to bury secretly. His job done, he goes off to fetch "the skeleton frame" and carries it to the grave. But his torch upsets, rolls into the grave, and is extinguished; and Nightgall, the corpse in his arms, is left in total darkness:

His first impulse was to throw down the body, but having, in his agitation, placed the hands, which were clasped together, over his neck, he found it impossible to free himself from it. His terror was so great that he uttered a loud cry, and would have fled, but his feet were rooted to the spot. He sank at last on his knees, and the corpse dropped upon him, its face coming into contact with his own. Grown desperate, at length, he disengaged himself from the horrible embrace, and threw the body into the grave. Relieved by this step from much of his fear, he felt about for the spade, and having found it, began to shovel in the mould.

While thus employed, he underwent a fresh alarm. In trampling down the mould, a hollow groan issued from the grave. Trembling in every limb, he desisted from his task. His hair stood erect, and a thick damp gathered on his brow. Shaking off his terrors, he renewed his exertions, and in a short time his task was completed.

He then groped his way out of the vault, and having become by long usage familiarised with its labyrinths, soon reached the entrance, where he struck the light, and having found a lantern, set fire to the candle within it. This done, he returned to the vault, where, to his great horror, he perceived that the face of the corpse was uncovered. Averting his gaze from it, he heaped the earth over it, and then flattened the mass with repeated blows of the spade. (II, xvi)

One of Ainsworth's motives in making the description of Alexia's interment so explicit was unquestionably to heighten the reader's sense of Nightgall's brutality; but, since there is plenty of other evidence for that, we conclude that Ainsworth rather enjoyed dwelling on such details for their own sake.

III *The Supernatural and the Foreordained*

The supernatural is found almost everywhere in Ainsworth's novels, particularly those set in more remote periods. Devils, ghosts, witches, and spirits abound, as do prophecies, spells, curses, and omens which never disappoint. With one interesting exception, to be noted later, Ainsworth commonly deals with these phenomena at face value and does not attempt to provide natural explanations for them: the supernatural is presented straightforwardly, without apology, as one dimension of the world he describes.

In this world, we quickly learn, everything is predetermined. Our sense of this is particularly strong, as we have noted, in Ainsworth's historical novels, in which our knowledge of what really happened to certain figures unavoidably affects our reactions to the sayings and doings of their fictional incarnations. In *Windsor Castle,* knowing what we do about English history, we cannot simply dismiss Catherine of Arragon's "malediction" of Anne Boleyn as the ranting of a demented woman:

"You suffer now, minion, but how will you feel when, in your turn, you are despised, neglected, and supplanted by a rival—when the false glitter of your charms having passed away, Henry will see only your faults—and will open his eyes to all I now tell him? ... You will have merited your fate; and will then think upon me and my woes, and will bitterly, but unavailingly, repent your conduct. And now, Henry," she exclaimed, turning solemnly to him, "you have pledged your royal word to me, and given me your hand upon it, that if you find this woman false to you, she shall expiate her offence on the block. I call upon you to ratify the pledge in her presence."

"I do so, Catherine," replied the king. "The mere suspicion of her guilt shall be enough."

"Henry!" exclaimed Anne.

"I have said it!" replied the king.

"Tremble, then, Anne Boleyn!" cried Catherine, "Tremble! and when you are adjudged to die the death of an adulteress, bethink you of the queen you have injured" (IV, i).

In *The Constable of the Tower,* in dealing with a somewhat less well known character, Ainsworth also reminds us again and again that, just as the real Thomas Seymour did not succeed in gaining the power he coveted, so the protagonist of the novel, despite his temporary triumphs, can come to no good end. Seymour is warned early in the novel by his mortal adversary, the Earl of Surrey:

"Now mark my words, for I feel they are prophetic. You and your brother have brought me to the scaffold—but my blood shall fly to heaven for vengeance. Your ambitious schemes shall come to nought. You shall have power only to lose it. The seeds of dissension and strife are already sown between you, and shall quickly grow and ripen. You shall plot against one another, and destroy one another. His hand shall sign your death-warrant, but your dying curse shall alight upon his head, and the fratricide shall perish on the same scaffold as yourself. Think on my words, Sir Thomas, when, like me, you are a prisoner in the Tower" (I, v).

There are many similar instances of foreshadowing throughout, and the conclusion of *The Constable of the Tower,* one very much in accord with Surrey's predictions, arouses no surprise.

A third historical novel, *The Leaguer of Lathom,* is particularly rich in forecasts of doom. At the very outset, the protagonist—Lord Strange, soon to become Earl of Derby—is much disturbed to see drops of blood falling on the book he is reading. It is "the disastrous year 1642"; the Civil War has just begun; and there is no doubt that the blood is an ominous portent (I, i). Shortly after this opening scene, Lord Strange's dying father, the sixth Earl of Derby, joins Strange's domestic chaplain in warning him against taking up arms in King Charles's cause: "It seems to me that I can look into the future, and I have a sad foreboding that all your possessions will be taken from you, and that a tragical death awaits you" (I, iii). In the following chapter, we are told that "an ill omen" attended the first display of the royal standard over Nottingham Castle: "Reared on the castle during a storm it was speedily blown down; nor could it be set up again till the fury of the storm had abated, when it was placed on the keep." Thus warned early in the novel (and, of course, mindful of the actual course of history), the reader cannot react with unqualified relief when the parliamentary siege of Lathom House, which forms the heart of the narrative, is finally lifted: the Royalist forces do ultimately go down to defeat; and, as we have been led to expect, the seventh Earl of Derby is martyred at Bolton, the scene of one of his earlier triumphs.

As we might anticipate, from what—for want of a better term—might be called Ainsworth's "world view," and from the fictional conventions to which he subscribed along with such more distinguished contemporaries as Dickens, coincidences abound in Ainsworth's novels: not perverse, random occurrences in an absurd, Hardyesque world, but structured events in a universe governed by a superintending Providence. This characteristic is to be remarked as clearly in his relatively few novels with Victorian settings as in those laid in the past.

Some examples from two of his later, less well known, novels, *Myddleton Pomfret* and *Hilary St. Ives,* illustrate his characteristic practice in this regard. Myddleton's wife, who might have chosen any place in England (or outside England, for that matter) as a refuge from the villain who is pursuing her, just happens to find a haven with a Mrs. Carew, who lives not far from where Pomfret's ward is staying; when the two young women strike up a friendship, Eva Bracebridge learns of her guardian's dishonorable past. Sir Norman Hylton just happens to learn of this same villain's nefarious designs on a third young woman because a servant accidentally substitutes a letter from the villain for another in Hylton's coat pocket: this provides the only possible means whereby those designs may be foiled. Neither of these events is, strictly speaking, a chance occurrence, though the modern reader might dismiss them as mere artifice; both form parts of a pattern, a design, which should not seem strange to anyone who knows how Ainsworth habitually regards the flow of events.

The hand of Providence—or "fate," as it is repeatedly called in the novel—is likewise seen everywhere in *Hilary St. Ives.* In a contemporary novel as full of Ainsworthian devices as any historical romance, the supposed Hilary St. Ives is in fact Aleric Delacombe, son of Colonel Seymour Delacombe and the woman who serves under the name of Mrs. Sutton as housekeeper to a Mr. and Mrs. Radcliffe at Hazlemere. It was fate, we are told, which brought Mrs. Sutton to the home of the woman whom Colonel Delacombe courted after he supposed his wife drowned; fate which led Mr. Radcliffe to give Aleric shelter at Hazlemere after he had been set upon and wounded by robbers; fate which decreed Colonel Delacombe's timely return from India, at first to help complicate and then to help unravel the plot. In a novel in which fate is thus constantly being referred to, we are disposed to listen when a gypsy soothsayer tells young May Radcliffe that she will mary Aleric, despite the fact that she is betrothed to another; and we take seriously the omens of death which come to two of the leading characters. All this evidence of the workings of Providence, it should be emphasized, occurs in a novel set in the 1860s against fashionable Victorian backdrops in which George Eliot's Daniel Deronda or Henry James's Isabel Archer would have felt thoroughly at home.

In such novels as *Windsor Castle, The Constable of the Tower,* and

The Leaguer of Lathom, Ainsworth exploited our knowledge of history to heighten the effect of the ominous prophecies he was so fond of using. In other instances, those involving different kinds of portentous pronouncements about the future, we also soon learn to give credence to the utterances of certain supernaturally endowed characters. The action of both *Rookwood* and *The Lancashire Witches,* for example, depends on curses about which we learn very early in the narrative; understanding as we do that such curses are never idly delivered in Ainsworth's fictional world, we helplessly watch characters about whom we care, more or less, become subject to their workings.

Just as such curses are genuine and have a binding effect, so other supernatural phenomena in Ainsworth's novels are objectively *there,* and are not simply the fabrications of highly excitable minds. It is possible to argue, for instance, that the protagonist of *Guy Fawkes* is a gloomy, brooding fanatic, convinced that Heaven has charged him with carrying out the gunpowder plot in order to restore the Roman Catholic church in England, and that the visions he keeps seeing are a consequence of his unbalanced mental state. Fawkes is certainly a fanatic and something of a mystic, but the fact remains that the narrative is not given from his point of view; the novel contains strange occurrences which are beheld by others and which could not, therefore, be dismissed as results of Fawkes's aberrations. For instance, a bell mysteriously and inexplicably tolls every time the conspirators begin digging their tunnel under Parliament: they all hear it. When, early in *Guy Fawkes,* Doctor Dee, the necromantic warden of the Manchester Collegiate Church, resurrects the prophetess Elizabeth Orton in order to have her predict the failure of the conspiracy, Fawkes is the only participant in the scene aside from Dee, Elizabeth, and Dee's assistant; but the incident is presented in such a manner that there can be no doubt about its objective equivalence to any other episode in the novel.

None of Ainsworth's novels is more redolent of the supernatural than, understandably, *The Lancashire Witches.* Several of the principal characters—the Demdikes, the Devices, Alice Nutter, Mother Chattox, Nan Redferne—actually are witches; all the others—Alizon, the Asshetons—are threatened by witches in some way. Witches terrorize the countryside and freely perform their eerie rites, and nothing in Ainsworth's account indicates that real witches were not as much a part of rural life in Jacobean England as the May Day revels with which the novel opens.

Nevertheless, there are some interesting and characteristically Ainsworthian inconsistencies in his treatment of the subject. Early in the novel, we are led to believe that the persecution of so-called witches is all a matter of ignorance and superstition. As Nicholas Assheton very plausibly puts it:

"the common folk hereabouts are blindly and foolishly superstitious, and fancy they discern witchcraft in every mischance, however slight, that befalls them. If ale turn sour after a thunder-storm, the witch hath done it; and if the butter cometh not quickly, she hindereth it. If the meat roast ill the witch hath turned the spit; and if the lumber pie taste ill she hath had a finger in it. If your sheep have the foot-rot—your horses the staggers or string-halt—your swine the measles—your hounds a surfeit—or your cow slippeth her calf—the witch is at the bottom of it all. If your maid hath a fit of the sullens, or doeth her work amiss, or your man breaketh a dish, the witch is in fault, and her shoulders can bear the blame" (II, iv).

There is also good sense in Alice Nutter's remark that King James's well-known belief in the existence of witches has resulted in a marked increase in their supposed prevalence: "men seek them out to win his favour." The very character to whom she says this, the witch-hunting and sycophantic attorney Potts, seems to be living proof of her hypothesis; and we sympathize with Mistress Nutter's fear that James's "sanguinary enactment" against witches, especially when carried out by the likes of Potts, "will put power into hands that will abuse it, and destroy many guiltless persons. It will make more witches than it will find" (II, iv).

Thus primed, we are prepared to sympathize with Nan Redferne, who is seized as a suspected witch and roughly handled by a mob which subjects her to the ordeal by water. As soon as the rope that supports her is allowed to go slack, "the poor woman" instantly sinks; she would have drowned had Richard Assheton not jumped into the Calder River to save her. Vindicated in this way, Nan is nevertheless much the worse for her experience, as Ainsworth points out in some detail: "Her thumbs were blackened and swollen, and the cords had cut in the flesh, while blood trickled down from the puncture in her breast. Fixing a look of inexpressible gratitude upon her preserver, she made an effort to speak but the exertion was too great; violent hysterical sobbing came on, and her senses soon forsook her" (II, vi). When Richard denounces the inhuman barbarity of the crowd, we cannot help agreeing with him. As for Nan, she is obviously innocent: did she not sink?

Ironically, however, we later discover that the pitiful Nan *is* a witch; so, we learn, is Alice Nutter, who is so wise, so rational, and so eloquent when she explains why people have allowed themselves to be whipped up into such a frenzy about witches. Ainsworth does not maintain what strikes the twentieth-century reader as his quite compelling social realism in treating witchcraft; instead, he quickly pulls all the stops as we move into the main action of *The Lancashire Witches.*

When Ainsworth turns from the past to his own times, of course, the atmosphere of his work changes drastically. But deeply ingrained habits die hard. *Old Court,* which has a mid-Victorian setting and the usual trappings of a novel of fashionable English county life, is full of distinctly Gothic overtones: the whole plot depends on a fratricide (which takes place in a "weird and fantastic" cromlech [Prologue, vi]); the gloom of the guilt-stricken murderer casts a pall over the whole action; and his chief antagonist and would-be blackmailer dies horribly in a fire that consumes a wing of the neo-Gothic Old Court. The room in which Sir Hugh Chetwynd was shot is supposed to be haunted by his ghost; but that mysterious presence turns out to be Sir Hugh's assassin, who returns to the scene of the crime for his own nefarious ends.

In Ainsworth's next novel, *Myddleton Pomfret,* the action of which also takes place in the nineteenth century, there is another haunted room in a dilapidated old country house. We are—rather pointlessly, it turns out—told about the legend, dating back to the time of James I, which accounts for the presence of the ghost; but the ghost herself never appears and the fact that the room is haunted has no significant bearing on the plot. *Chetwynd Calverley,* another novel with a contemporary setting, is marked by several supernatural incidents, including a portent of evil: according to an old legend, a piece of black oak rises to the surface of Brackley Mere whenever something dreadful is to happen in the Barfleur family; and, immediately following such an occurrence, Sir Leycester Barfleur is killed while pursuing two gypsy robbers.

In the semi-autobiographical *Mervyn Clitheroe,* fun is poked—uniquely among Ainsworth's novels—at those who believe in supernatural phenomena. The rascally barber-surgeon Pownall keeps manufacturing such manifestations in order to fleece the credulous old Hazilrigge, and the reader does not take them seriously for a moment as soon as he suspects what Pownall's game is. This instance is not the only one, however, in which *Mervyn Clitheroe* serves as the uncharacteristic exception to the Ainsworthian rule, which in this case might run as follows: in the usual Ainsworth novel, set in remote ages, he indulges freely in whatever supernatural effects he believes will help him advance action, establish character, or heighten mood, and he has no qualms whatever about presenting them without, or contrary to, any kind of rational explanation. They are simply and unapologetically a part of his violent world.

CHAPTER 5

Dramatis Personae

I *General Characteristics*

NOT even the most sympathetic reader of Ainsworth's novels would deny the element of truth in Malcolm Elwin's charge that Ainsworth's characters are "almost always sterile or stereotyped." [1] We have only to recall his invincible heroes, like Crichton; his virtuous heroines, like Lady Jane Dudley; his hard-luck protagonists, like Thames Darrell—figures, all of them, who either come through adversity unruffled and unblemished or—less often—serenely die the death of the just and the pure. On the other end of the moral scale, there are the many deep-dyed villains whose evil natures are tempered by no saving touch of humanity. Between these extremes, there are hundreds of characters who are little more than names, descriptions, attributes—characters who are quickly forgotten.

We find no Sam Wellers, no Becky Sharps, no Heathcliffs, no Maggie Tullivers, no Jude Fawleys in Ainsworth; for real originality is totally lacking among his dramatis personae. Even in so uncharacteristic a novel as *Mervyn Clitheroe,* the cast is comprised of stock figures: the titular hero, rather more appealing than most of Ainsworth's young men, seems to be—how consciously no one can, of course, say—a nineteenth-century reincarnation of Tom Jones, forever good-naturedly blundering into mishaps; and Malpas Sale, Mervyn's adversary, a wily, smooth, and ruthless young hypocrite, is just as obviously a latter-day Master Blifil.

In most of Ainsworth's work, a few basic types recur among his fictional—as opposed to his historical—characters. The protagonist, a meritorious young man who has to make his way in the world against great odds, is frequently forced to recover his birthright from those who have wrongfully deprived him of it. He is in love with a chaste maiden who is subjected to a series of threats ranging from the inconvenient (parental disapproval of her love) to the unspeakable (loss of "honor"). Even more than the young hero, the young heroine is held to a strict code of sexual morality: premarital and extramarital involvements are not countenanced, and those who violate this code invariably suffer great remorse and either social ostracism or early death. The adulteresses in Ainsworth's last two novels, Mrs. Aylmer Mallet in *Beau Nash* and Aline Heyrick in *Stanley Brereton*, have duels fought over them; after one of the antagonists dies, each woman takes religious vows, withdraws from the world, and tries to atone for her sin by prayer and good works. Jane Shore, the adulterous paramour of Edward IV in *The Goldsmith's Wife,* meets with a miserable end; and even the innocent Amabel Bloundel, who falls victim to the Earl of Rochester's lechery in *Old Saint Paul's,* cannot be restored to respectable society and consequently must be killed off by her creator.

As a general rule, however, the heroine manages to preserve her virtue; and she and the hero (and usually one or more other happy couples as well) are united at the end in matrimony. This happy ending occurs in spite of the worst efforts of the novel's villain, who lays snares to trap the worthy young people and who is usually straight out of nineteenth-century melodrama, as indeed are the minor character types who keep appearing: various categories of servants—faithful, faithless, mischievous, sinister, or clownish; rakes and playboys active, redeemed, or unredeemable; lawyers and doctors—benevolent or crafty; clergymen—saints or bluff and hearty men of the world or canting hypocrites; moneylenders; innkeepers; and so on.

Ainsworth's handling of character is unquestionably inept in several respects. He is, for instance, excessively fond of complicating characterization by the use of mistaken identities: someone behaves in a manner inappropriate to his station, and it is ultimately discovered that his real station is quite different from what it appears to be. Alan Rookwood in *Rookwood,* the Princess of Condé and Ginevra Malatesta in *Crichton,* Constance Sheppard in *Jack Sheppard*, Angela Mountjoy in *The Tower of London,* Lady Isabella Argentine in *Old Saint Paul's,* Mabel Lyndwood in *Windsor Castle,* Alizon in *The Lancashire Witches,* and Lady Amicia Wilburton in *Mervyn Clitheroe* are among the most prominent examples. Sometimes these false identities are deliberately assumed; in other instances, they stem from mysteries of parentage of which the characters involved are themselves unaware. In either case, Ainsworth resorts to this tired device so frequently that its use takes on the aspect of an obsession.

In one novel, *The Flitch of Bacon,* most of the principal characters bear false names: Doctor Plot, who has also been known as John

Johnson, is really the unhappy Sir Walter Fitzwalter; Frank Woodbine and his wife Rose turn out to be the offspring, respectively, of Sir Walter and Squire Mark Monkbury; Squire Monkbury's supposed niece, Bab Bassingbourne, is in fact his daughter; the enormous Captain Juddock has assumed a variety of roles at fairs—Plinlimmon, the Welsh giant; Pennigant, the Yorkshire giant; Tregonna, the Cornish giant—and at one point in his career he becomes a Moslem and calls himself Amurath the Turk.

Ainsworth's characters don and doff disguises with the greatest of ease and with a high degree of effectiveness. Perhaps the extreme example of this facility occurs in *Tower Hill,* when Francis Dereham so contorts his features and alters his posture as to assume a new identity, that of Hugh Tilney, secretary to Catherine Howard. He plays this role without the benefit of makeup or costume.

Just as Ainsworth tends to be inconsistent in the handling of other elements of his novels, so his treatment of certain characters often seems to vacillate. In these cases, we are not concerned with the complexity of human behavior, which does tend to vary considerably from moment to moment in all but the most dully stable of us, but with certain contradictions and ambiguities which leave Ainsworth open to the charge of negligence or even forgetfulness. Some examples are helpful in establishing this point.

In *Guy Fawkes,* it is difficult to be certain about the motivation of one of the chief conspirators, Robert Catesby. Catesby is in love with Viviana Radcliffe, the daughter of a rich Catholic landowner in Lancashire. She, however, is strongly attracted to Fawkes. Catesby is jealous of Fawkes for this reason, and he is furious with Fawkes because Fawkes has broken up a forced marriage between Catesby and Viviana by giving Viviana proofs that Catesby already has a wife. Humiliated and frustrated, Catesby vigorously swears to withdraw from the gunpowder plot; at his next appearance, nevertheless, he resumes his role of arch-conspirator and never again either mentions or shows his animosity to Fawkes.

A more serious problem in a less spectacular novel has to do with the characterization of old Scarve, the miser, in *The Miser's Daughter.* Ainsworth's preface makes it appear that the novel is going to be some sort of pious moral tract: "To expose the folly and wickedness of accumulating wealth for no other purpose than to hoard it up, and to exhibit the utter misery of a being who should thus surrender himself to the dominion of Mammon, is the chief object of these pages." Avarice, obviously, is a subject with endless possibilities for the imaginative writer; and a Molière or a Balzac can show it manifesting itself in many ways in the same individual. But with Ainsworth, miserliness is a matter of now one thing, now another, with no unity or coherence in our response to the character concerned. It is difficult to know whether to despise Scarve, feel sorry for him, or laugh at him. At different times we do all three, and his gruesome death—"unattended, in a cellar, half entombed in the hole digged as a hiding-place for a portion of his wealth" (III, xi)—is out of keeping with the matter-of-fact mood of the rest of the novel, even though it does underscore the theme enunciated in the preface.

Scarve, at least, is a reasonably consistent character: it is the situations into which he is thrust, and the ways in which he is made to react to them, that vary. Quite another problem occurs in the characterization of Increase Micklegift, the Puritan minister in *Ovingdean Grange,* who cannot seem to decide with which party in the English Civil War to throw in his lot: basically, of course, his allegiance is to the Roundheads, but he loves Dulcia Beard, the daughter of the Royalist clergyman whom he has displaced, and he hates the Puritan officer Stelfax, whom he rightly regards as his rival for Dulcia's affections. Had it been possible, or worth Ainsworth's while, to give anything like full treatment to this unhappy man, his dilemma might have been made entirely credible and even effective; as it is, the reader finds it difficult to accept Micklegift's vacillation.

A similar problem arises in *The Constable de Bourbon.* Is the protagonist of that novel, set in France, Italy, and Spain in the 1520s, a wronged nobleman or is he a contemptible traitor? There is evidence on both sides, and Ainsworth—with a huge canvas to cover—does not really paint a clear enough picture of Bourbon to provide us with an answer.

Equally hard to explain is the sudden repentance of Felix Fairlie, the villain of *The Spendthrift.* The scheming corrupter of the protagonist for most of the novel, Fairlie suffers a seizure near the end after hearing of his daughter's death, and undergoes a "total revulsion": "he was just as eager to repair the wrongs he had committed as he had lately been to uphold them" (xlix). The fact that his dramatic conversion is totally unnecessary makes it even harder to accept: Fairlie's complicated plottings have brought him to the point where his exposure and the undoing of his villainous deeds are imminent anyway.

Some of Ainsworth's inconsistent characters, it should be added in all fairness, are rather more effectively done than Catesby, Scarve, Micklegift, Bourbon, and Fairlie; in *The Lancashire Witches,* Nicholas Assheton, the Puritan squire who engages in some un-Puritanical diversions and who combines superstition and common sense in a remarkable way, comes off quite well—as does, in the same novel, James I, who is by turns magnanimous and petty, royally stern and appealingly human.

In the main, however, Ainsworth was unquestionably prone to take the easy way out in his characterizations, and he was not above an occasional blunder. But it would be doing him an injustice simply to leave the matter at that. At his best, he was capable of bringing to his treatment of character the same sort of imaginative intensity which marked his handling of dramatic or visual scenes; and, even though he did not succeed in creating a whole gallery of unforgettable portraits, he certainly managed to fashion some compelling figures.

II *The Tormented Protagonist*

Three character types in Ainsworth's work stand out as particularly worthy of note. There is, in the first place, what might be called the tormented protagonist type, illustrated by such characters as Luke Rookwood, Jack Sheppard, and Guy Fawkes. Each of these characters is gifted and in some way attractive; each of them is driven by outside forces of whose true nature he is not fully aware to commit desperate deeds which grieve and horrify many of those near and dear to him; each experiences as much anguish as triumph in the course of his career; each is ultimately killed as a result of his ambition. There are, of course, crucial differences among them: the point to be stressed, however, is that each of them is somehow made to *live* by Ainsworth.

Perhaps the least successful of these three examples is Luke, whose desires are inflamed by the urgings of his fanatical grandfather. Reared by the gypsy Barbara Lovel, and destined to marry her granddaughter Sybil, Luke was apparently an uncomplicated, well-meaning young rustic until Alan Rookwood, for sinister motives of his own, began working on him. Luke's bitter reproach of old Rookwood for his gloomy vengefulness suggests how much Luke regrets the loss of his primal innocence:

"Peace," cried Luke; "you blight everything—even this smiling land-scape you would turn to gloom. Does not this morn awaken a happier train of thoughts within your mind? With me it makes amends for want of sleep, effaces resentment, and banishes every black misgiving. 'Tis a joyous thing, thus to scour the country at earliest dawn; to catch all the spirit and freshness of the morning; to be abroad before the lazy world is half awake; to make the most of brief existence; and to have spent a day of keen enjoyment, almost before the day begins with some" (III, i).

Luke's fundamental good nature also comes to the fore when he attempts to rescue Lady Rookwood, his father's second wife, from the robbers who menace her, despite the fact that she has shown herself to be his implacable enemy. Though he allows Alan Rookwood to maneuver him into a marriage with the unwilling Eleanor Mowbray, which means abandoning Sybil and depriving his half-brother Ranulph of his affianced bride, Luke is not without remorse at "the enormity of the cruel, dishonourable act" (III, xi).

Luke's agitation begins at the very outset of the novel when Alan, who has for many years played the role of a simple sexton, reveals to Luke that his mother was murdered at the behest of Sir Piers Rookwood.

"Am I the sport of this mocking fiend?" cried he, "to whom my agony is derision—my despair a source of enjoyment—beneath whose withering glance my spirit shrinks—who, with half-expressed insinuations, tortures my soul, awakening fancies that goad me on to dark and desperate deeds? " (I, i)

Luke's excitement naturally does not diminish when he discovers that Sir Piers had married his mother and that he is, therefore, heir to his father's estates, and his feelings are constantly exacerbated by the goading of the demented Alan.

By the time Luke makes his final appearance, he bears all too obvious signs of the suffering which he has endured in his new station in life:

Harassed and exhausted by the life he had recently led; deprived almost of natural rest; goaded by remorse, his frame was almost worn to the bone, while his countenance, once dark and swarthy, was now blanched and colourless as marble. . . . His dark eyes blazed with their wonted fire—nay, they looked darker and larger from his exceeding paleness, and such intense mental and bodily suffering was imprinted upon his countenance, that, despite its fierceness and desperation, few could have regarded him without sympathy. (V, iv)

Ainsworth's depiction of Luke fails for two main reasons to grip us fully. In the first place, the stage diction which Ainsworth puts into the young man's mouth is grossly inappropriate to one reared as Luke has been and is obviously, too obviously, designed to squeeze every last ounce of melodrama out of Luke's unhappy situation. In the second place, the reader is not really made familiar enough with Luke's nature to accept without question what Ainsworth repeatedly tells him: this is a soul in conflict and torment. Nevertheless, the main force of the hair-raising incidents in which Luke is continually involved sweeps us along, and we are willing to concede a good deal of what Ainsworth asks of us in our response to Luke.

A similar, but more effective, case is Jack Sheppard's. Jack is led to his life of crime by the machinations of Jonathan Wild and the harshness and callousness of Mrs. Wood. Thanks to his great physical agility and his ingenuity and resourcefulness, he becomes a master criminal; but, despite the depths of depravity to which he sinks, his better nature is never extinguished. This aspect constantly manifests itself in his feelings for Thames Darrell, Winifred, Mr. Wood, and especially his mother; and the yawning gulf between what he is—what he has allowed himself to become—and what he might have been—what others have desperately wanted him to be—causes him frequent anguish. Jack, unlike Luke Rookwood, is not given to theatrical outbursts of emotion; but there can be no doubt as to his remorse in such scenes, for instance, as his conversations with Mrs. Sheppard after his escape from Newgate and shortly before her death, and especially in his hair-raising encounter with her when she is an inmate in Bedlam. When Jack dies on the gallows at Tyburn, he is thoroughly remorseful and penitent.

The darker side in Jack, though undeniably present and important, is, however, only one facet of a complicated and, on the whole, rather attractive personality. To be sure, he is a robber; but there are worse sorts of criminals. He is loyal to those who have befriended him and is himself capable of inspiring great loyalty, as we see in Blueskin's attachment to him. Though he goes too far on occasion in his wenching and his drinking, he is no stranger to the ways of conviviality.

Quite different from Jack is Guy Fawkes, whose spiritual torments are relieved by no human diversions and whose very love for Viviana is of an ascetically self-denying sort. We know from the start that he is a monomaniac: "A soldier of fortune, but a stern religious enthusiast, he supposed himself chosen by Heaven for the redemption of his Church, and cared not what happened to himself, provided he accomplished his (as he conceived) holy design" (I, iii). Even when he is persuaded on impressive supernatural authority that his plot is doomed to failure, he resists Doctor Dee's suggestion that he abandon the conspiracy:

"Be warned, my son. You are embarked on a perilous enterprise, and if you pursue it, it will lead you to certain destruction."

"I cannot retreat," rejoined Fawkes, "and would not if I could. I am bound by an oath too terrible to be broken."

"I will absolve you of your oath, my son," said Doctor Dee, eagerly.

"You cannot, reverend sir," replied Fawkes. "By no sophistry could I clear my conscience of the ties imposed upon it. I have sworn never to desist from the execution of this scheme, unless those engaged in it shall give me leave. Nay, so resolved am I, that if I stood alone I would go on" (I, vii).

Constituted as he is, irrevocably wedded to an enterprise which cannot possibly succeed, Fawkes moves from grief to grief in the course of the narrative. That he is by far the most single-minded of the conspirators, and that there are several admirable characters—like Viviana, her father, and Humphrey Chetham—in the novel who absolutely oppose the plot, only heightens our sense of the hopelessness of Fawkes's position.

III *The Power-hungry Schemer*

A second interesting character type which recurs with some frequency in Ainsworth's novels is that of the power-hungry schemer— the figure who intrigues to gain and use power, not so much because of what power will bring him, but compulsively, for the very joy of exercising it. He may lurk in the shadows, busily pulling strings, like Catherine de Medicis in *Crichton,* Simon Renard in *The Tower of London,* Cardinal Wolsey in *Windsor Castle,* or Father Petre in *James the Second*; or, like Thomas Seymour in *The Constable of the Tower,* he may make a bold, direct bid for the titles and emoluments of power. In either case, this type of character seems energized by some superhuman urge which not only renders him remarkably effective but which also appears to deprive him of the scruples which would normally belong to someone in his position.

Perhaps the best representative of this type is Catherine de Medicis of *Crichton.* Utterly unprincipled, utterly ruthless, this "she-wolf Catherine" (I, vi), this "bloody Jezebel of France" (III, ii) is quite explicit about her motives: "The Salic law prevents the exercise of sovereign authority in my own person. I reign through my sons . . ." (III, v):

In her hands, her sons were mere puppets; they filled the throne, while she wielded the sceptre. Hers was truly, what it has been described, "a soul of bronze, or of iron." Subtle, secret, Machiavelian—the "Prince" of the plotting Florentine was her constant study—her policy worked in the dark: none could detect her movements till they were disclosed by the results. Inheriting many of the nobler qualities of the Medicis, her hatred was implacable as that of the Borgias: and, like that dread race, her schemes were not suffered to be restrained by any ties of affinity. Rumour attributed to her agency the mysterious removal of her two elder sons from the path of the third, who was unquestionably her favourite; and she was afterwards accused of being accessory to the death of another, the Duc d'Alençon, who perished at Chateau-Thierry, from smelling at a bouquet of poisoned flowers. (II, i)

When her son Henri III reigns, she attempts to rule him: she encourages his dissipations in order to keep him weak; she uses her *"petite bande des dames de la cour,"* who wield sex as their weapon, as agents and spies to consolidate her power and to discover the plots of her adversaries at court; and she chooses a spineless, feeble wife, Louise de Vaudemont, for Henri, so that no opposition to her will may come from that possibly dangerous quarter. When Henri grows "wayward and capricious" and "refuses to follow my counsels—to acknowledge my sway" (III, v), she schemes to have him assassinated and to replace him with his presumably more pliable brother, François de Valois, Duc d'Anjou. Having earlier sought to have Crichton poisoned, because he too stood in the way of her machinations, she attempts to enlist his aid in this nefarious enterprise by bribing him with the hand of the Princess of Condé (whom she has held in reserve for just such an emergency) and the baton of a marshal of France; but the peerless Crichton, needless to say, refuses to become a party to such treachery.

IV *The Unmotivated Villain*

A third and final type of character of which note should be taken is the unmotivated villain, the person who with great relish perpetrates wicked deeds simply for their own sake. Though such deeds may, and usually do, enhance his own position, that result is really beside the point: the zest with which he commits them indicates very clearly that, for him, evil is its own reward. The thief-taker Jonathan Wild in *Jack*

Sheppard, the jailer Nightgall in *The Tower of London,* and the plague nurse Judith Malmayns in *Old Saint Paul's*—all of whom have already been discussed—well exemplify this type; an ever better case in point, perhaps, because his malignity is so utterly without apparent purpose is Ugo Harrington, Sir Thomas Seymour's esquire in *The Constable of the Tower.*

A minor villain throughout the novel, Harrington does not reveal the full extent of his depravity until the story is nearly finished. During most of *The Constable of the Tower* he is Seymour's confidant and loyal servant; indeed, he goes far beyond the call of duty in carrying out missions for his master. When, for instance, he is sent to Princess Elizabeth with a letter from Seymour, he takes it upon himself to act as Seymour's advocate:

"Not only shall this letter be delivered to the adorable princess with the tresses of gold, which seem to have ensnared your Lordship, and which I must needs own are most ravishingly beautiful, but I will lose no opportunity of sounding your praises in her ear."

"Note her slightest word and look when thou speakest of me, Ugo, and report them."

"You shall have every blush, every downcast look, every half-sigh of the divinity faithfully rendered, monsignore. 'Tis a pity I cannot take my cittern with me, or I might sing her a love-strain which could not fail to move her. Luckily, the enchanting princess speaks Italian fluently, and if she will only encourage me, I will converse with her in that language of love, and then I shall be able to say more than I should dare utter in our rude northern tongue" (I, vii).

Ainsworth makes much of the fact, at every opportunity, that Harrington is half-Italian; quite possibly this nationality is intended to account for his un-English, Iago-like deviousness and malignity. Indeed, although Harrington gives his master no overt sign that he is not to be trusted, Elizabeth's suspicions are aroused by his ardor, and she says of him to Seymour:

"By my fay, a sprightly galliard! . . . and much devoted to you, I should judge. He could talk of little else save his lord's merits and noble qualities, and harped so much upon the theme, that I was obliged at last to bid him change it, or hold his tongue. . . . Methinks you make too great a confidant of this galliard. They of his country are proverbially faithless" (I, xi).

There is a brief, unexplained reference to Harrington's "malice" a chapter later; but, as far as anyone can see, he continues to serve Seymour well and imaginatively, listening patiently while the Lord High Admiral unfolds his ambitious schemes to him and carrying out faithfully Seymour's morally questionable orders. Indeed, Seymour is outstripped as a schemer by Harrington on at least one occasion: when Harrington argues that Catherine Parr (whom Seymour has by then married) has outlived her usefulness and should be got out of the way, preferably by poison, Seymour recoils in horror from the suggestion; but Harrington poisons her anyway. On her deathbed, Catherine, who suspects Harrington, reproaches Seymour for employing Harrington as her murderer: "What motive could Ugo have for my destruction? Why should he desire my death? He is merely your instrument" (III, iii). In fact, however, this is one crime of which Seymour is innocent, even technically: Harrington has simply been carried away by his wicked exuberance.

Soon after this incident Harrington, for no apparent reason, turns against Seymour. (There is a mysterious allusion to some great hurt which Seymour is alleged to have done Harrington in the past, but it is never explained, nor is it ever made clear why Harrington waits until sixty pages from the end of the novel to break faith with his master.) Just as Harrington had formerly served Seymour with great energy, so he now moves vigorously in betraying Seymour's plot to seize the Tower, providing Seymour's enemies with a complete list of his secret allies, and personally arresting Seymour in the name of the Lord Protector and the council. When Harrington calls on Seymour to yield himself a prisoner and deliver up his sword, no one can blame Seymour for his response.

"Take it to thy heart, vile traitor!" cried Seymour, plunging his rapier with such force into the esquire's body that the hilt smote against his breast. Uttering a fearful cry, Ugo fell backwards, and, unable to keep his seat in the saddle, rolled heavily to the ground, where he lay, breathing against his slayer. (III, x)

No one could claim that Ainsworth ranks with Shakespeare or Dickens as a prolific inventor of remarkable characters, or with Jane Austen or Thackeray as a psychologist. No one could quarrel with the assertion that his characters, on the whole, are stock figures, either frozen immobile in fixed postures or given to wildly inconsistent alterations. It seems undeniable, however, that Ainsworth at his best can energize his characters by thrusting them into inherently dramatic situations, that he can infuse them with the vitality that marks so much of his writing, that he is at his best in depicting the desperate, the power-mad, and the malign—that he can, in short, wring from even the most reluctant reader a response, however grudging, to the actions and the passions of his people.

CHAPTER 6

Voices

I *General Characteristics*

BEFORE the "disappearance of the author" into anonymity, which Joseph Warren Beach singles out as a prominent characteristic of modern fiction,[1] a novelist was likely to make his presence felt everywhere in his works; he more or less baldly lectured his reader, chided or praised his characters, and generally made no secret of his prejudices and predilections. No writer in the century and a half which marked the golden age of the English novel was less reticent than William Harrison Ainsworth about intruding his own personality and his own views. Everywhere in his novels we hear what we soon come to recognize as his distinctive voices. This observation is certainly and obviously true of his expository passages; but it is even noticeable to the reader moderately familiar with Ainsworth's work in scenes which are rendered dramatically.

As we might expect from a writer who deals so extensively with architectural or topographical settings, Ainsworth frequently assumes the role of guide, pointing out—much as some kinds of handbook would—the distinctive features of the physical background which he is attempting to establish. A passage chosen almost at random from *The Tower of London* is typical:

Proceeding along the ascent leading towards the green, and mounting a flight of stone steps on the left, we arrive in front of the ancient lodgings allotted to the Lieutenant of the Tower. Chiefly constructed of timber, and erected at the beginning of the sixteenth century, this fabric has been so much altered, that it retains little of its original character. In one of the rooms, called, from the circumstance, the council chamber, the conspirators concerned in the Gunpowder Plot were interrogated; and in memory of the event, a piece of sculpture, inscribed with their names, and with those of the commissioners by whom they were examined, has been placed against the walls. (II, iv)

102

A number of Ainsworth's most elaborate descriptive passages deal with natural as well as man-made settings. A passage near the opening of *Windsor Castle* is typical for its use of detail (and for its reference, in the second paragraph, to the nineteenty-century aspect of the scene described); less usual is the fact that the panorama is viewed by a specific character (in this case the Earl of Surrey) rather than by the omniscient author:

On his right stretched the broad green expanse, forming the Home Park, studded with noble trees, chiefly consisting of ancient oaks, of which England had already learnt to be proud, thorns as old, or older than the oaks, wide-spreading beeches, tall elms, and hollies. The disposition of these trees was picturesque and beautiful in the extreme. Here, at the end of a sweeping vista, and in the midst of an open space, covered with the greenest sward, stood a mighty, broad-armed oak, beneath whose ample boughs, though as yet almost destitute of foliage, while the sod beneath them could scarcely boast a head of fern, couched a herd of deer; there lay a thicket of thorns skirting a sand-bank, burrowed by rabbits; on this hand, grew a dense and Druid-like grove, into whose intricacies the slanting sunbeams pierced; on that, extended a long glade, formed by a natural avenue of oaks, across which, at intervals, deer were passing. . . .

On the left, a view altogether different in character, though scarcely less beautiful, was offered to the gaze. It was formed by the town of Windsor, then not a third of its present size, but incomparably more picturesque in appearance, consisting almost entirely of a long straggling row of houses, chequered black and white, with tall gables and projecting stories, skirting the west and south sides of the castle; by the silver windings of the river, traceable for miles, and reflecting the glowing hues of the sky; by the venerable college of Eton, embowered in a grove of trees; and by a vast tract of well-wooded and well-cultivated country beyond it, interspersed with villages, churches, old halls, monasteries, and abbeys.

Similarly, as befits a historical novelist, Ainsworth often fills in historical background, much as a popular chronicler would:

Two years before, namely in 1663, more than a third of the population of Amsterdam was carried off by a desolating plague. Hamburgh was also grievously afflicted about the same time, and in the same manner. Nothwithstanding every effort to cut off communication with these states, the insidious disease found its way into England by means of some bales of merchandise, as it was suspected, at the latter end of the year 1664, when two persons died suddenly, with undoubted symptoms of the distemper, in Westminster. Its next appearance was at a house in Long Acre, and its victims two Frenchmen, who had brought goods from the Levant. (*Old Saint Paul's,* I, i)

There are countless set pieces in Ainsworth's historical novels describing in minute detail not only the physical appearance of his characters but also their dress and every aspect of the ceremonial occasions in which they participated, such as processions, pageants, and especially (Ainsworth must have been exceedingly fond of the pleasures of dining and drinking well) banquets. Aside from their frequency, length, and specificity, two things are striking about these passages: the enormous amount of social-historical research that must have gone into them, and (usually) their tendency to slow down the action of the novels in which they are included. Even in the best intentioned reader, fully alive to Ainsworth's rich descriptive power, the temptation to skip or skim such passages occasionally becomes overwhelming.

A few examples indicate the range of Ainsworth's usual practice in this regard. In the opening chapter of *The Tower of London,* Lady Jane Dudley and her entourage proceed by barge from Durham House to the Tower. The vessels in which they travel are carefully described, as are their crews:

a squadron of fifty superbly-gilt barges,—some decorated with banners and streamers,—some with cloth-of-gold and arras, embroidered with the devices of the civic companies,—others with innumerable silken pennons to which were attached small silver bells, "making a goodly noise and a goodly sight as they waved in the wind,"—while others, reserved for the more important personages of the ceremony, were covered at the sides with shields gorgeously emblazoned with the armorial bearings of the different noblemen and honourable persons composing the privy council, amid which the cognizance of the Duke of Northumberland,—a lion rampant, *or,* double quevée, *vert,*—appeared proudly conspicuous. Each barge was escorted by a light galley, termed a foist or wafter, manageable either by oar or sail as occasion demanded, and attached to its companion by a stout silken tow-line. In these galleys, besides the rowers, whose oars were shipped, and in readiness to be dropped, at an instant's notice, into the tide, and the men-at-arms, whose tall pikes, steel caps, and polished corslets flashed in the sunbeams, sat bands of minstrels provided with sackbuts, shalms, cornets, rebecs, and other forgotten musical instruments.

Ainsworth lavishes similar detail on his account of the royal procession:

The advanced guard ... was formed by a troop of halberdiers dressed in striped hose of black and tawny, velvet caps decked at the side with silver roses, and doublets of murrey and blue cloth, embroidered on the front and at the back with the royal blazon, woven in gold. Their halbert staves were covered with crimson velvet, fastened with gilt nails, and ornamented with golden tassels. Filing off on the right and left, they formed two long lines, extending from the gateway of the palace to the foot of the plank communicating with the barge nearest the shore. A thick rayed cloth was then unfolded, and laid down between them by several attendants in the sumptuous liveries of the Duke of Northumberland. This done, a flourish of trumpets resounded from within; a lively prelude arose from the musicians on the water; and two ushers with white wands marched at a slow and stately pace from the portal. They were followed by an officer bearing the mace; after whom came another carrying the sword of state; then several serjeants of the city guard, in their full accoutrements, and with badges on their sleeves, then the garter king-at-arms in his tabard; then several knights of the Bath, each having a white lace on his sleeve; then their esquires; then the judges, in their robes of scarlet and coifs; then the Bishop of Ely, who, in his character of Lord High Chancellor, wore a robe of scarlet, open before, and purfled with miniver, then the aldermen, likewise in cloaks of scarlet; the sheriffs; and, finally, the lord mayor, Sir George Beame, in a gown of crimson velvet, and wearing the collar of SS.

Sufficient time having been allowed for the embarkation of these important personages, who, with their attendants, filled several barges, another flourish of trumpets was heard, fresh symphonies resounded from the river, and the heads of the different civic companies in their robes of state, descended and departed.

The reader is left in no uncertainty concerning the appearance of the principal participants in this initial scene of *The Tower of London.* Cranmer, Archbishop of Canterbury, and Ridley, Bishop of London, "were attired in the scarlet simar, and surplice with its snowy lawn sleeves, proper to their order." The twelve gentlemen attending Antoine de Noailles, the French ambassador, wore "splendid habiliments, consisting of pourpoints of white damask, barred with gold, short mantles of crimson velvet, lined with violet taffeta, and carnation-coloured hauts-de-chausses." The attendants of the Spanish ambassador, Simon Renard, are more austerely garbed "in suits of black velvet, entirely without ornament." Renard himself is described more in terms of his character than his apparel: he

was as plainly attired as his followers, his sole decoration being the Toison d'Or: but of all that brilliant assemblage, perhaps there was none so likely to arrest and rivet attention as this remarkable man; and as he is destined to play no inconsiderable part in this history, it may be worth while to take a narrower survey of his personal appearance. Somewhat above the middle height, and of a spare but muscular frame, he had a dark complexion, rendered yet more sombre in its colour from the contrast it presented to his grizzled beard and moustaches. His eye was black and flaming, his nose long and hooked, and he had a stern searching glance, which few could withstand. There was something mysterious both in his manner and character which made him universally dreaded; and as he never forgave an offence, nor scrupled at any means of gratifying his vengeance, it was not without reason that he was feared. A subtle politician and skillful diplomatist, high in the favour of the most powerful sovereign in Europe, with apparently inexhaustible funds at his command; inexorable in hatred, fickle in friendship, inconstant in affairs of gallantry, suspected of being mixed up in every political intrigue or conspiracy, Simon Renard had been for some time the terror and wonder of Edward's court, and had been regarded with suspicion and jealousy by Northumberland, who looked upon him as a dangerous opponent.

The "haughty and disdainful" Duke of Northumberland, the new queen's father-in-law,

was habited in a doublet of white satin, with a placard or front-piece of purple cloth of tissue, powdered with diamonds and edged with ermine. Over this he wore a mantle of cloth of silver, pounced with his cipher, lined with blue velvet, set with pearls and precious stones, and fastened with a jewelled clasp. From his neck was suspended the order of the Garter, while in his hand he carried the silver verder belonging to his office as grand-master of the realm.

The queen's father, the Duke of Suffolk, "was scarcely less magnificently arrayed, in a doublet of black cloth of gold, and a cloak of crimson satin, flowered with gold, and ribanded with nets of silver." Finally, Jane herself appears, accompanied by her consort:

Her dress consisted of a gown of cloth-of-gold raised with pearls, a stomacher blazing with diamonds and other precious stones, and a surcoat of purple velvet bordered with ermine. Her train was of purple velvet upon velvet, likewise furred with ermine, and embroidered with various devices in gold. Her slender and swan-like throat was encircled with a carcanet of gold set with rubies and pearls, from which a single and almost priceless pearl depended. Her head-dress consisted of a coif of velvet of the peculiar form then in vogue, adorned with rows of pearls, and confined by a circlet of gold. At her right walked Lord Guilford Dudley—a youthful nobleman, who inherited his father's manly beauty and chivalrous look, with much of his ambition and haughtiness, but without any of his cunning and duplicity, or of his genius. He was superbly attired in white cloth-of-gold, and wore a collar of diamonds.

One of the more elaborate banqueting scenes in Ainsworth is the grand dinner given in honor of James I by Sir Richard Hoghton in *The Lancashire Witches.* Again, Ainsworth goes to great lengths in setting the scene:

The *coup-d'oeil* of the banquet-hall on the monarch's entrance was magnificent. Panelled with black lustrous oak, and lighted by mullion windows, filled with stained glass and emblazoned with the armorial bearings of the family, the vast and lofty hall was hung with banners, and decorated with panoplies and trophies of the chase. Three long tables ran down it, each containing a hundred covers. At the lower end were stationed the heralds, the pursuivants, and a band of yeomen of the guard, with the royal badge, a demi-rose crowned, impaled with a demi-thistle, woven in gold on their doublets, and having fringed pole-axes over their shoulders. Behind them was a richly carved oak screen, concealing the passages leading to the buttery and kitchens, in which the clerk of the kitchen, the pantlers, and the yeomen of the cellar and ewery, were hurrying to and fro. Above the screen was a gallery, occupied by the trumpeters and minstrels; and over all was a noble rafter roof. The tables were profusely spread, and glittered with silver dishes of extraordinary size and splendour, as well as with flagons and goblets of the same material, and rare design. The guests, all of whom were assembled, were out-numbered by the prodigious array of serving-men, pages, and yeomen waiters in the yellow and red liveries of the Stuart.

Flourishes of trumpets announced the coming of the monarch, who was preceded by Sir Richard Hoghton, bearing a white wand, and ushered with much ceremony to his place. At the upper end of the hall was a raised floor, and on either side of it an oriel window, glowing with painted glass. On this dais the King's table was placed, underneath a canopy of state, embroidered with the royal arms, and bearing

James's kindly motto, *"Beati Pacifici."* Seats were reserved at it for the Dukes of Buckingham and Richmond, the Earls of Pembroke and Nottingham, the Lords Howard of Effingham and Grey of Groby, Sir Gilbert Hoghton, and the Bishop of Chester. These constituted the favoured guests. Grace having been said by the bishop, the whole company took their seats, and the general stillness hitherto prevailing throughout the vast hall was broken instantaneously by the clatter of trenchers.

A famous feast it was and worthy of commemoration. Masters Morris and Miller, the two cooks who contrived it, as well as the labourers for the ranges, for the pastries, for the boiled meats, and for the pullets, performed their respective parts to admiration. The result was all that could be desired. The fare was solid and substantial, consisting of dishes which could be cut and come to again. Amongst the roast meats were chines of beef, haunches of venison, gigots of mutton, fatted geese, capons, turkeys, and sucking pigs; amongst the boiled, pullets, lamb, and veal; but baked meats chiefly abounded, and amongst them were to be found red-deer pasty, hare-pie, gammon-of-bacon pie, and baked wild-boar. With the salads, which were nothing more than what would now-a-days be termed "vegetables," were mixed all kinds of soused fish arranged according to the sewer's directions—"the salads spread about the tables, the fricassees mixed with them, the boiled meats among the fricassees, roast meats amongst the boiled, baked meats amongst the roast, and carbonadoes amongst the baked." This was the first course merely. In the second were all kinds of game and wild-fowl, roast herons three in a dish, bitterns, cranes, bustards, curlews, dotterels, and pewits. Besides these there were lumbar pies, marrow pies, quince pies, artichoke pies, florentines, and innumerable other good things. Some dishes were specially reserved for the King's table, as a baked swan, a roast peacock, and the jowl of a sturgeon, soused. These and a piece of roast beef formed the principal dishes. (III, ix)

Less obviously related to the kind of fiction he characteristically wrote is Ainsworth's repeated insistence on explicitly judging the figures in his novels: not with tongue-in-cheek irony, like that displayed by Thackeray and Trollope on similar occasions, not with the compassionate penetration of a George Eliot, but tersely, straightforwardly, in terms of black and white moral criteria. As we have seen, Ainsworth suggests quite clearly, in a number of ways, what we are to think of the more important characters in his novels; about the lesser ones, there can usually be no doubt whatever, because he flatly tells us.

Regarding Henry VIII, for example, we are given our signals at the very beginning of *The Constable of the Tower*: "Rapacious and cruel, and lavish as rapacious, his greediness was insatiable. . . . Crafty as well as resolute, he framed laws merely to deride and break them." Because the author must resort to this kind of shorthand here, and because his judgment of Henry is that which is commonly held, Ainsworth is on quite safe ground in this case; less acceptable, however, is his frequent interruption of the narrative in order to censure or to excuse the actions of his characters. In the same novel, when Catherine Parr finally yields to Sir Thomas Seymour's passionate suit and agrees to marry him, Ainsworth instructs us how we are to react: "She knew the character of the man who sought her hand. Yet she agreed to a sudden and secret marriage with him. Her love overmastered her discretion. Some excuse may be found for her in the resistless manner and extraordinary personal attractions of her suitor. Few of her sex would have come off scathless from the ordeal to which she was subjected" (II, iv).

On occasion, Ainsworth goes even beyond this kind of advocacy, as in his summary judgment of the Penderel brothers in *Boscobel*: "Their part in our story is played. Yet before dismissing them, we would express our genuine admiration of the loyal men we have endeavoured to depict. . . . The Penderel brothers were men of unwavering loyalty, brave as faithful, possessed of such extraordinary strength as rendered them truly formidable antagonists. . . . Very pleasant it has been to chronicle their actions, and we part from them with regret" (IV, vi).

Like a number of classic English novelists, though Ainsworth went about it less skillfully than the best of them, he was fond of inserting little moral essays into his narratives. Here, for instance, is the opening of Epoch the Second of *Jack Sheppard*:

TWELVE years! How many events have occurred during that long interval! How many changes have taken place! The whole aspect of things is altered. The child has sprung into youth; the youth has become a man; the man has already begun to feel the advances of age. Beauty has bloomed and faded. Fresh flowers of loveliness have budded, expanded, died. The fashions of the day have become antiquated. New customs have prevailed over the old. Parties, politics, and popular opinions have changed. The crown has passed from the brow of one monarch to that of another. Habits and tastes are no longer the same. We, ourselves, are scarcely the same as we were twelve years ago.

Twelve years ago! It is an awful retrospect. Dare we look back upon the darkened vista, and, in imagination, retrace the path we have trod? With how many vain hopes it is shaded! with how many good resolutions, never fulfilled, is it paved! Where are the dreams of ambition in which, twelve years ago, we indulged? Where are the aspirations that fired us—the passions that consumed us then? Has our success in life been commensurate with our own desires—with the anticipations formed of us by others? Or, are we not blighted in heart, as in ambition? Has not the loved one been estranged by doubt, or snatched from us by the cold hand of death? Is not the goal, towards which we pressed, farther off than ever,—the prospect before us cheerless as the blank behind? Enough of this. Let us proceed with our tale.

II *Some Stylistic Quirks*

Ainsworth the guide, Ainsworth the chronicler, Ainsworth the judge, Ainsworth the moralist—all these roles which our author is fond of assuming quickly become familiar as we get to know his work. Certain quirks of style and diction, too, soon come to strike us as distinctively Ainsworthian.

He is inordinately given to the dangling modifier, for example, as some of the quotations in this study (most recently the description of Henry VIII from *The Constable of the Tower* quoted on p. 109) may have suggested. His characters are forever "making the best of their way" somewhere or, when wounded, exhausted, or badly frightened, finding that "their limbs refuse their office." Exclamatory expressions abound, with "Soh!" perhaps the most frequent and certainly the tersest. Ainsworth also can be precious and arch: in *Old Court,* which reads in places as if Ainsworth had enrolled in the silver-fork school, the romantic affliction of a young officer is described in these words: "the blind god had winged his keenest shaft up to the feather in the gallant captain's heart" (I, i); a pair of youthful lovers on horseback are "enamoured equestrians" (VI, ii); and so on. When he attempts to be lyrical, he often succeeds only in sounding strained, resembling nothing so much as one of Thackeray's parodies of his contemporaries' excesses:

Animate nature was just beginning to feel the quickening influence of the God of Day. The garrulous occupants of the higher trees made the welkin ring with their cawing as they flew past in quest of their morning meal; lesser birds twittered amongst the boughs; the mavis burst from the holm-tree to dispute the first worm upon the grass plot with the intrusive starling; pigeons were circling around the house, or alighting on the roof; lowings of oxen and other noises resounded from the farm-yard; and the tinkling of the sheep-bell was heard on the adjacent down, where might be seen the fleecy company, just released from the fold, in charge of the shepherd, and looking as grey as the turf on which they browsed. (*Ovingdean Grange*, II, ii)

In addition to such verbosity, inflation, and circumlocution, Ainsworth's language is often marked by the mock antiquity of Wardour Street English. In a historical novel like *The Constable of the Tower* we come upon chapter titles such as this: "How the Right High and Renowned King Henry the Eighth waxed grievously Sick, and was like to Die" (Prologue, I); and upon speeches like "'Tis horrible to think that a foul and murtherous caitiff should disfigure a god-like frame like yours, and sever such a head from such a frame! No—no—it cannot—shall not be" (Princess Elizabeth speaking, IV, iii) or "Vindictive wretch! thou hast well deserved thy fate! ... Remove the body to Mauger's vault yonder—beneath the Bloody Tower.... And let these sanguinary stains be effaced.... Now, bring on the prisoner. To the palace!" (Sir John Gage speaking, III, x).

Ainsworth's efforts at historical verisimilitude in his dialogue are frequently painful. A sixteenth-century French king speaks to his jester, who has just sung a particularly clever song:

"Gramercy ... thou hast fairly earned thy hippocras, were it only for the justice rendered to the lovely Esclairmonde, who, as thou truly sayest, outshines all. But, by our lady, messeigneurs, we must not neglect the service of Bacchus for that of Apollo. Samson, thy choicest Cyprus—a health! " (*Crichton*, II, vii)

And a seventeenth-century Puritan fumes with moral outrage (which, Ainsworth suggests, was perpetual among Cromwell's adherents in the Civil War):

"What! thou perfidious and dissembling Episcopalian, hast thou entrapped our leader, a mighty man of valour like Amasiah, the captain of Jehoshaphat, and fastened him within yon closet? Give me the key thereof instantly, or I will smite thee with the edge of the sword, even as the false priests of Baal were put to death by the soldiers of Jehu" (*Ovingdean Grange*, IV, v).

III *Melodramatic Features*

Whole chapters in any number of Ainsworth's novels might, with very little change, have made effective scenes in Victorian melodramas. There are, for example, many passionate confrontations, couched in highly emotional language, between hero and villain, with the honor of the virtuous heroine at stake. Typical in this regard is Chapter XI of Book II of *Cardinal Pole,* in which Philip of Spain, who has amorous designs on Constance Tyrrell, forces her to choose whether her lover's life or her own chastity is to be sacrificed:

". . . you are wholly in my power. Nothing can deliver you. On your decision hangs your lover's life. You—you will cause his immediate arrest—his imprisonment, torture—ay, torture—and death."

"Oh, say not so, Sire!" she cried, all her firmness deserting her. "What has he done to deserve such barbarous treatment?"

"He has dared to disobey me," rejoined Philip. "He has stepped between me and the object of my desires. But for your sake I am content to forego revenge—nay, to heap greater favours on his head. Will you cast him into a dungeon? Will you doom him to torture and death?"

"I cannot save him by the sacrifice you propose, Sire," she rejoined, in tones of anguish. "Neither would he consent to be so saved."

"You have avouched the truth, Constance," exclaimed Osbert, springing through the open window, and placing himself between her and the King. "A thousand deaths rather than such a sacrifice."

Comparable to Osbert's timely and dramatic entrance is the appearance—on the stage, we are tempted to say—moments later of a zealous Protestant who has already made one attempt on Philip's life. Like Osbert, he precipitates a quick change of mood:

"At last you are beginning to comprehend your true position," observed Philip, in a taunting tone, "and perceive that you are utterly without help."

"Not utterly," cried a deep voice. And Derrick Carver strode into the room. "Heaven will not desert them in their need. Thou hast uttered threats against them which thou wilt never live to execute. Thou hast ventured into this dwelling, but wilt never return from it. My hand failed me when I first struck at thee, but it will not fail me now."

"Make the attempt, then, if thou think'st so, assassin!" cried Philip, keeping his eye steadily upon him.

"Hold! " exclaimed Osbert. "His life is sacred."

The chapter continues at this pitch for several additional pages.

Even in a novel with a nineteenth-century setting like *Mervyn Clitheroe,* dialogue and action are often more reminiscent of the stage than of real life, as in this excerpt from a scene in which a mother chastises her daughter in the presence of the girl's brother:

"Have I reared you—have I toiled for you—have I paved your way to fortune—ungrateful, disobedient child, only to find you turn upon me thus? But tremble! Your ingratitude and disobedience warrant me in invoking condign punishment upon your head."

And as she spoke she raised her arm, as if about to pronounce a malediction. Affrighted at the gesture, Apphia flung herself at her feet, and clasped her knees.

But Mrs. Brideoake was held in check by one who had never before asserted supremacy over her. For the first time in his life her son turned a menacing and indignant look upon her, and she gazed upon him, as all who beheld him did, in astonishment and awe.

John seemed endowed with superhuman power, and drawing up his tall figure to its full height, he regarded his mother with eyes that flashed with lightning.

"Forbear, mother! " he exclaimed, stretching out his hand towards her. (II, xv)

Such dramatic devices as the aside and the soliloquy are also commonly found in Ainsworth's fiction. In *John Law,* they are used in conjunction with another, which occurs in practically every one of the novels: the concealed observer listening in on an important conversation meant to be secret. The scapegrace Raoul Laborde overhears his father telling a trusted servant where he has hidden a large hoard of money from the agents of the Chamber of Justice. "What is this I hear? " says Raoul, as the two old men are talking. "A hundred thousand livres concealed in the cellar! " The conversation is repeatedly interrupted by such ejaculations, which the audience hears but which old Laborde and the servant do not; and, when they withdraw, Raoul comes forward and says:

"A precious discovery I have made! . . . I always suspected my father had a secret hoard, but I never fancied the amount so great as a hundred thousand livres. I will denounce him at once. Yet hold! 'tis an execrable act I am about to commit—worse than robbery. Pshaw! the money is of no use to the miserly old hunks, since he daren't spend it, while to me it will be everything. What if I conceal myself in the house, and carry off the chest, or one of the money-bags they spoke of. No, that won't do. If caught, I should be sent to the galleys, whereas by pursuing the other course I shall be screened and rewarded, and, best of all, the denunciation can be made in a feigned name. So away with all foolish scruples" (II, i).

Clearly, Ainsworth had no intention of disappearing from his narratives. Nor, having decided to obtrude himself, was he capable of the irony, the wit, the profundity, the subtlety, or the humor which the sophisticated modern reader tends to look for in authorial commentary. He was, rather, straightforward and matter-of-fact—traits which were probably welcome and helpful to his large nineteenth-century audience. In his dramatic scenes, too, he eschewed psychological nuances and fidelity to everyday habits of speech, drawing instead in big, bold, obvious strokes. The voices of Harrison Ainsworth address us as from the podium or across the flickering footlights; but, if we abandon some of our modern prejudices about the proper language of fiction and surrender ourselves to the spell which he attempts to cast, these voices often reach us with surprising clarity and power.

Conclusion

WHAT, then, is the twentieth-century reader to make of the novels of Harrison Ainsworth? If that reader looks to Ainsworth for well-wrought plots and memorable characterizations, he is likely to suffer disappointment. If he seeks subtlety of technique and finely shaded nuances in the fiction he admires, he will not find them in Ainsworth. If he has little patience with the stock conventions of the classical English novel, he will be repelled by a great deal in Ainsworth's cliché-ridden books.

He may, however, discover some surprising compensations in these dusty volumes. As what used to be called, rather condescendingly, "escape" literature, they are unsurpassed, capturing in each novel a crowded, swarming, teeming, self-contained world. Whereas the contemporary novelist is likely to offer his reader a thin, pale, chilled, slightly acrid fictional broth, Ainsworth sets down before him a steaming, bubbling, thick and hearty stew, redolent of exotic seasonings and full of strange, unexpected chunks and morsels.

But the modern reader who comes to Ainsworth to scoff and who then stays to lose himself in his fictional world may learn something else before he returns to the real world. Hopelessly antiquated though much of Ainsworth is, he nonetheless knew a good deal about some aspects of human nature which we often prefer to forget. Man's craving for power—latent in all of us, an obsession in some—has been better understood by only a handful of novelists. How power is won; and, once won, how it is exercised are subjects to which Ainsworth returns again and again: how one man—or, less often, a faction—comes to dominate a court and a whole country. Conversely, he also shows how loss of power over oneself and others can bring a man to ruin: a very painful sort of ruin, generally, because Ainsworth is under no illusion about the mercy and charity which we are wont to extend to our fellows.

If Ainsworth's world is full of surface pomp and pageantry and a sense of continuity and tradition which runs rather deeper, it is nevertheless cruel and violent at the core—a truth, quite possibly, which makes it all the more imperative to retain what we can of ceremony and convention and what little there may be of human compassion. More than the general run of nineteenth-century novelists and more than even many writers of our own day, Ainsworth was aware of the irrational side of human nature and of the drives, the hopes and fears, to which it gives rise. The modern reader—recognizing the shrewdness of this insight, and eventually coming to appreciate the skill with which Ainsworth renders his world view—may well concede that much in Ainsworth engages the highest powers which he is capable of bringing to the fiction he reads.

Appendix:
Concise Synopses of Ainsworth's Novels

(The dates given in parentheses are those of book publication.)

Sir John Chiverton (1826). Though Sir John Chiverton has established himself as the owner of Chiverton Hall, the rightful owner is in fact Sir John's sister Ellice. Reginald Prestwyche (Ellice's lover and Sir John's enemy) reveals this secret to Sir Gamelyn de Vancouver, father of Isabel, Sir John's intended; but, with the aid of the wicked physician Walter Scymel, Sir John is able to allay Sir Gamelyn's misgivings. Ellice helps Reginald escape from the dungeon in which Sir John has imprisoned him, but she dies while running away from her brother, who, she thinks, means to kill her. Both Sir John and Scymel die at Sir John's wedding feast from poison administered by the cruel Moor Mahmood Bali.

Rookwood (1834). On the death of Sir Piers Rookwood, three great questions are raised. Who shall succeed to his estate: Ranulph, his son by Lady Rookwood; or Luke, his son by Susan Bradley, to whom, as it turns out, Sir Piers was secretly married, thus making Luke, who is older than Ranulph, legitimate and his heir? Which of the brothers shall marry Eleanor Mowbray, the heiress of Sir Piers's father Sir Reginald Rookwood? What is to become of Sybil Lovel, Luke's gypsy sweetheart, whom he abandons in order to pursue Eleanor? With the help of his supposed grandfather, the crazed sexton Peter Bradley (in reality Alan Rookwood, Sir Reginald's wronged brother), and of the highwayman Dick Turpin, Luke nearly succeeds in his goal, but he is mortally poisoned when he kisses a strand of the dead Sybil's hair which her old grandmother, the gypsy queen Barbara Lovel, has sent him. Ranulph and Eleanor are united, and the curse on the house of Rookwood is lifted when Lady Rookwood finds the dagger with which the founder of the family stabbed his wife to death.

Crichton (1837). See Chapter 2, pp. 55-56.

Jack Sheppard (1839). See Chapter 2, pp. 53-55.

117

The Tower of London (1840). See Chapter 2, pp. 60-61.

Guy Fawkes (1841). The novel is Ainsworth's fictionalized account of the gunpowder plot of 1605, the motives and difficulties of the conspirators, the failure of their desperate plan, and their subsequent sufferings and executions. Ainsworth introduces a strong attraction between Fawkes and Viviana Radcliffe, daughter of a Catholic landowner in Lancashire. She is strongly opposed to the plot, and attempts to dissuade Fawkes from pursuing it; after its failure, she tries to move him to repentance.

Old Saint Paul's (1841). Leonard Holt, a grocer's apprentice, loves his master's daughter, Amabel Bloundel. She is relentlessly pursued by the Earl of Rochester, who finally succeeds in abducting her from a house in Kingston Lisle where she has gone to recover her health after an attack of the plague. Leonard befriends a girl he knows as Nizza Macascree, a poor piper's daughter, but who is really Lady Isabella Argentine. She falls in love with Leonard while he is still in love with Amabel, but his feeling for her grows, especially after Amabel's death. As soon as her true identity is discovered, a match between Isabella and Leonard seems to be out of the question, but Leonard wins the favor of King Charles II, having saved the monarch's life during the great fire of 1666 and devised a scheme to halt the spread of the conflagration; he is given a title and the king's support, and all obstacles to the marriage are removed.

The Miser's Daughter (1842). See Chapter 2, p. 49.

Windsor Castle (1843). See Chapter 2, pp. 47-48.

Saint James's (1844). A relatively plotless and formless novel, this deals with the power struggles surrounding Queen Anne in the last seven years of her reign, chiefly the successful Tory attempt, led by Harley and St. John, to eliminate the influence of the Duchess of Marlborough and bring disgrace on her husband, the Duke. At Anne's death, both these ringleaders, now the Earl of Oxford and Viscount Bolingbroke, respectively, are at odds with each other and fallen from favor.

James the Second (1848). Like several of Ainsworth's later historical novels, this one takes place on two levels. At the public level, we see the downfall of King James II, the successful revolution of 1688, and the invasion of England by William of Orange. At the private level, we are asked to concern ourselves with the romance between Charles Moor, a young gentleman loyal to James, and the Huguenot Sabine Saint Leu.

Their union becomes possible after Charles finds means to prove that he is really the rightful bearer of the title of Lord Mauvesin and the false Lord Mauvesin dies horribly as the London mob sets fire to the house of the Spanish ambassador.

The Lancashire Witches (1849). See Chapter 2, pp. 48-49.

The Star-Chamber (1854). During the reign of James I, the racketeers Sir Giles Mompesson and Sir Francis Mitchell enrich themselves by a variety of extortionate schemes and cause much suffering to their victims who come to be judged by the Star Chamber. The fortunes of the Mounchesney family, which they have ruined, are rehabilitated: Jocelyn, son of Sir Ferdinando Mounchesney, recovers the family estates and is put in a position to marry Aveline Calveley.

The Flitch of Bacon (1854). Perhaps the most prominent among a tangle of ill-related plot strands concerns the contest between two country couples for the Dunmow Flitch of Bacon, a token of married bliss.

The Spendthrift (1857). Goaded on by his rascally steward Fairlie, who grows rich at his young master's expense, Gage de Monthermer ruins himself by gambling and extravagant living. Just as he is about to displace Gage completely, Fairlie has a change of heart consequent on the death of his daughter Clare, and, shortly before he himself dies, restores his fortune to the penitent and reformed Gage.

Mervyn Clitheroe (1858). See Chapter 2, pp. 49-50.

Ovingdean Grange (1860). After the battle of Worcester in 1651, Clavering Maunsel takes refuge at Ovingdean Grange, the Sussex house of his father, Colonel Maunsel, a staunch royalist. The young man is ultimately captured by the wily captain of the Ironsides, Stelfax, but manages to escape with his friends from the village church in which they have been held prisoner. From that point on, a little more than half way through the novel, the emphasis shifts to Charles Stuart and his entourage and their efforts to elude the Parliamentary forces. After a period of hiding at Ovingdean Grange, Charles makes his way to Shoreham, where he sets sail for France. Before that, he persuades Colonel Maunsel to withdraw his objections to a match between Clavering and Dulcia Beard.

The Constable of the Tower (1861). See Chapter 3, p. 66.

The Lord Mayor of London (1862). Like *The Spendthrift,* this novel concerns the reformation of an extravagant young eighteenth-century man-about-London, Tradescant Lorimer, son of the Lord Mayor, who, after numerous crises, settles down to respectability, now worthy of marrying his Yorkshire cousin Prue and willing to carry on his father's business as a draper.

Cardinal Pole (1863). Another bilevel novel, this one deals with the intricacies and intrigues of English history from the arrival of Philip of Spain at Southampton to the death of Mary Tudor, and also with the ill-fated romance of Osbert Clinton, a Protestant conspirator, and Constance Tyrrell, the object of Philip's unwelcome attentions.

John Law (1864). Law was a Scottish financier active for a time at the French court in the early eighteenth century. His seemingly miraculous schemes, involving paper money, credit, and the establishment of the Bank of France, prosper briefly and then crash disastrously. The subplot—involving the capitalist Laborde, his daughter Colombe, and his dissolute son Raoul—shows how the speculative fever incited by Law wrecks the fortunes and lives of one family.

The Spanish Match (1865). The first Charles Stuart travels to Madrid in 1623 to claim the Infanta Maria as his bride. He has many adventures en route; once in Spain, he is frustrated in his hopes of bringing off the match, chiefly because of the religious difference between himself and the Spanish princess, but also because of the machinations of his adviser Buckingham and King Philip's adviser Olivarez.

Auriol (1865). Certainly the most disjointed of Ainsworth's novels and probably unfinished, this is the story of Auriol Darcy, a young Elizabethan who dreams (or did it really happen?) that he kills his great-grandfather, an alchemist who goes by the name of Dr. Lamb, in order to possess himself of the "elixir of life" which enables him to live on into the nineteenth century, subject from 1800 on to a curse which requires that he deliver up every ten years a woman he loves to the devil, otherwise known as Rougemont.

The Constable de Bourbon (1866). Charles de Bourbon holds the high position of Constable of France but quarrels with his king, François I, and leads an army against him. François is defeated at the battle of Pavia but is released by Charles V after the treaty of Madrid. Bourbon himself dies at the head of a force which is about to sack Rome. His motives are never clearly established; and, possibly because of this and possibly because of the diffuse structure of the novel, which rambles all over western Europe between June, 1523, and May, 1527, this is one of Ainsworth's least successful ventures into historical fiction.

Old Court (1867). Here, in a contemporary setting, Ainsworth has produced a curious mixture of genres: a novel of fashionable county life, a melodrama, a Gothic tale. Having accidentally murdered his brother Clarence, Sir Hugh Chetwynd gives his property to the dead man's son, young Clarence, when he appears at Old Court many years after his father's death. Young Clarence loves Lucetta, Sir Hugh's daughter, but she loves Captain Rainald Fanshaw and contrives a match between Clarence and Fanshaw's sister. The sole surviving witness of the senior Clarence's murder is Neal Evesham, alias Vandeleur La Hogue; he blackmails Sir Hugh, then kills him, and finally perishes himself in a fire at Old Court.

Myddleton Pomfret (1868). Burdened by heavy debts, Julian Curzon pretends to drown himself in Lake Windermere in full view of his horrified bride, Sophy. In fact he goes off to India to make his fortune under the name Myddleton Pomfret. Believing herself to be a widow, Sophy marries the infamous Captain Scrope Musgrave, who knows Myddleton is Sophy's husband and who has insulted Myddleton's ward Eva Bracebridge. Musgrave ultimately turns his attention to Tiffany Flaxyard, but his plot is foiled by Sir Norman Hylton, who loves Eva Bracebridge, and Musgrave is killed by Pomfret in a duel.

Hilary St. Ives (1870). The young artist Hilary St. Ives turns out to be Aleric Delacombe, the long-lost son of Colonel Seymour Delacombe and the supposed Mrs. Sutton (really Barbara Ilminster), housekeeper to the Radcliffes at Hazlemere. When his true parentage and station are revealed, all obstacles to his union with May Radcliffe are removed.

The South-Sea Bubble (1871). Like *John Law,* this novel treats financial speculation on a massive scale, though in England rather than France. Ainsworth lays bare the political and fiscal scheming behind the "blowing" of the famous bubble and its bursting in 1720. At the private level, the parentage of Margaret Harpledown, whose father was killed by robbers, is established; she recovers his will from his murderers and marries her true love, Trevor Craven.

Tower Hill (1871). Catherine Howard captures the affections of Henry VIII just as he marries his fourth queen, the plain Anne of Cleves. Henry divorces Anne and marries Catherine, not knowing that she had betrothed herself as a girl to another. Catherine becomes involved in the power struggles between the Protestant and Catholic parties, using her influence over Henry in the Catholics' behalf; but after the Protestant Archibishop Cranmer tells Henry of her betrothal and her supposed infidelity with another man, the king condemns her to death.

Talbot Harland (1871). The titular hero, a member of King Charles II's court, is rather a cipher. Though he finally marries his lady love, Dorinda Neville, he achieves no great exploits and suffers some reverses, particularly in his dealings with the highwayman Claude Duval, who goes by the alias of Count de Bellegarde. For the rest, the novel is an ill-organized account of Duval's feats, the designs of Colonel Blood on the Duke of Ormond and the crown jewels, the king's amours, and court manners.

Boscobel (1872). See Chapter 2, p. 61.

The Manchester Rebels of the Fatal '45, published as *The Good Old Times* (1873). A group of prominent Manchester men join the cause of Prince Charles Edward during the Jacobite rising of 1745. When the rebellion is put down, they pay with their lives for their loyalty to the Stuarts. A happy exception is Atherton Legh, really Conway Rawcliffe, dispossessed of his birthright by his uncle Sir Richard Rawcliffe, who later restores it to him. Conway is pardoned by the Duke of Cumberland at the intercession of another uncle, Colonel Conway, marries his cousin Constance Rawcliffe, and lives happily ever after at Rawcliffe Hall.

Merry England (1874). Chaucer is one of the characters in this account of Wat Tyler's rebellion and its suppression. There is some slight story interest in the fate of Editha, believed to be the daughter of Wat Tyler, who is in fact the child of noble parents.

The Goldsmith's Wife (1875). When Jane Milverton is a young girl, it is foretold that she will have a royal lover. Later, after she is married to the goldsmith Alban Shore, she captures the fancy of King Edward IV. He makes her his mistress, and she comes to wield great influence at his court. After his death, Jane tries, unsuccessfully, to help Edward's widow protect his sons from Gloucester (later Richard III), who has them put to death in the Tower. Jane herself dies in poverty and disgrace.

Preston Fight (1875). This novel deals with an episode in the Jacobite revolt of 1715, the defeat of the rebels at the siege of Preston. Though several of their leaders escape from the Tower, one of the most admired, the Earl of Derwentwater, is beheaded for his role in the rebellion.

The Leaguer of Lathom (1876). One of King Charles's most loyal supporters during the Civil War is the Earl of Derby, though his services to the crown are not always properly requited. Equally gallant is his wife, the Countess of Derby, who defends Lathom House against the Parliamentary forces in the Earl's absence. The novel—not one of Ainsworth's better constructed efforts—ends with Derby's martyrdom at Bolton, seven years after the main action.

Chetwynd Calverley (1876). The protagonist's stepmother, Teresa Calverley, poisons his father, and makes herself mistress of his fortune. Refusing to accept any favors from Teresa, Chetwynd leaves home. He tries suicide and briefly considers going into service as a footman. Teresa wants to marry Lord Courland and attempts to poison her stepdaughter Mildred, to whom her property would go in the event of her marriage. She fails in this design, and, stricken with remorse, kills herself. The novel ends to the peal of wedding bells: Chetwynd, safely back home by now, marries his sweetheart, and three other happy couples are joined in matrimony.

The Fall of Somerset (1877). Most of this novel, a kind of sequel to *The Constable of the Tower,* deals with the power struggle between the Duke of Somerset and the Earl of Warwick, later Duke of Northumberland, during Edward VI's reign. Somerset is disgraced and stripped of his office of Lord Protector. When he makes his peace with Northumberland, he temporarily regains some of his honors, only to lose them all again, and his life, after he resumes his plotting. There is also a rather inconclusive romance between Augustin Stewart, who plays an ambiguous role in the public action of the novel, and Margaret Flowerdew, daughter of a rapacious Norfolk landowner. She twice nurses Edward VI back to health but dies of consumption before she can marry Augustin.

Beatrice Tyldesley (1878). King James II has been deposed and, after his defeats in Ireland, has retired to Saint-Germain. His adherents try, unsuccessfully, to restore him to the throne. Beatrice Tyldesley is a Jacobite who becomes maid of honor to Queen Mary of Modena at Saint-Germain. Walter Crosby, her lover, is also attached to the Jacobite cause, though circumstances twice take him to the court of William and Mary. Beatrice and Walter are united in marriage after much unexplained delay.

Beau Nash (1879). The "Beauty of Bath," Mrs. Aylmer Mallet, elopes from her husband with Sir Thomas Carew. After Carew kills Mallet in a duel, she leaves him, enters a religious retreat as Sister Helena, and eventually dies there. Mallet's nephew, Frank Farington, with the aid of

Beau Nash, woos and eventually wins the once coquettish Edith Wilmot, overcoming the objections of both mothers.

Stanley Brereton (1881). Sir Thomas Starkey is killed in a duel by Lionel Darcy, cousin of Lady Starkey, whom Sir Thomas has wronged by running off to Dieppe with another woman, Aline Heyrick. His nephew, Stanley Brereton, succeeds to his property. Stanley marries the flirtatious Mildred Warburton, who later elopes with Darcy. Stanley kills Darcy in a duel. Mildred falls ill but recovers and is taken back by her loving father and husband. When she is killed in a fall from a horse, Stanley becomes free to marry Rose Hylton, whom he has grown to love.

Notes and References

Chapter One

1. S. M. Ellis, *William Harrison Ainsworth and His Friends* (London, 1911), I, 21. Subsequent references to Ellis in the first section of Chapter 1 are given in parentheses in the text. This initial section draws very heavily on Ellis.

2. *Cf.* below, p. 37.

3. The growth of the eighteenth-century reading audience is usefully charted in the second chapter of Richard D. Altick, *The English Common Reader* (Chicago, 1957), pp. 30–66.

4. Quoted in Kathleen Tillotson, *Novels of the Eighteen-Forties* (London, 1954), p. 15.

5. Walter Allen quotes P. H. Newby to the effect that Maria Edgeworth may have been a more important novelist than Jane Austen and implies agreement with Newby. *The English Novel* (New York, 1957), p. 107.

6. Altick, p. 81.

7. Altick, p. 290.

8. Altick, p. 383.

9. Quoted by Amy Cruse, *The Englishman and His Books in the Early Nineteenth Century* (London, 1930), p. 229.

10. Ellis, I, 145–46.

11. John Marriott, *English History in English Fiction* (New York, 1941), p. 9.

12. Lionel Stevenson, *The English Novel* (Boston, 1960), p. 25.

13. Ellis, I, 25.

14. Editor's Introduction to [John Leland,] *Longsword* (New York, 1957), ed. John C. Stephens, Jr., p. vii.

15. Anthony Trollope, *Autobiography,* quoted in Tillotson, p. 141.

16. Preface to Horace Walpole, *The Castle of Otranto* (London, 1923), p. xlvii.

17. Montague Summers, *The Gothic Quest* (London, n.d.), pp. 191–92.

18. Frank W. Chandler, *The Literature of Roguery* (Boston, 1907), I, 3.

19. Chandler, I, 1—2.
20. Keith Hollingsworth, *The Newgate Novel* (Detroit, 1963), p. 3.
21. Hollingsworth, in his definitive study of this kind of novel, establishes 1830—1847 as the period within which it flourished.
22. G. M. Young, *Victorian England* (New York, 1954), pp. 55—57.
23. Quoted in Hollingsworth, p. 93.
24. Hollingsworth, p. 132.
25. Hollingsworth, p. 145.
26. The passage is represented in Appendix B of Geoffrey and Kathleen Tillotson's edition of *Vanity Fair* (Boston, 1963), p. 672.
27. Matthew W. Rosa, *The Silver-Fork School* (New York, 1936), p. 8.
28. Ellis, I, 255—56.
29. Michael Booth, *English Melodrama* (London, 1965), p. 13.
30. Allardyce Nicoll, *A History of English Drama* (Cambridge, 1955), IV, 102.
31. *Ghiotto* was published in Arliss's *Pocket Magazine*, VIII (1821), 181—89, 250—57.
32. VII (1821), 292—94.

Chapter Two

1. Ainsworth claimed that it "was completed in one day and one night," a feat involving "the composition of a hundred ordinary novel pages in less than twenty-four hours." Ellis, I, 236.

Chapter Three

1. See, e.g., Ellis, I, 178—181.

Chapter Four

1. See Ellis, I, 230—31, on the genesis of *Rookwood*. Ainsworth said, among other things, that he "resolved to attempt a story in the bygone style of Mrs. Radcliffe (which had always inexpressible charms for me)."

Chapter Five

1. Malcolm Elwin, *Victorian Wallflowers* (London, 1934), p. 174.

Chapter Six

1. Joseph Warren Beach, *The Twentieth Century Novel* (New York, 1932), p. 14.

Selected Bibliography

PRIMARY SOURCES

Sir John Chiverton. London: Ebers, 1826.
Rookwood. London: Routledge, 1878.
Crichton. London: Routledge, 1879.
Jack Sheppard. London: Routledge, 1879.
The Tower of London. London: Routledge, 1878.
Guy Fawkes. London: Routledge, 1878.
Old Saint Paul's. London: Routledge, 1879.
The Miser's Daughter. London: Routledge, 1879.
Windsor Castle. London: Routledge, 1878.
Saint James's. London: Routledge, 1879.
James the Second. London: Colburn, 1848. 3 volumes.
The Lancashire Witches. London: Routledge, 1878.
The Star-Chamber. London: Routledge, 1879.
The Flitch of Bacon. London: Routledge, 1879.
The Spendthrift. London: Routledge, 1879.
Mervyn Clitheroe. London: Routledge, 1879.
Ovingdean Grange. London: Routledge, 1879.
The Constable of the Tower. London: Routledge, 1880.
The Lord Mayor of London. London: Routledge, 1880.
Cardinal Pole. London: Routledge, 1880.
John Law. London: Routledge, 1881.
The Spanish Match. London: Routledge, 1880.
Auriol. London: Routledge, 1881.
The Constable de Bourbon. London: Routledge, 1880.
Old Court. London: Routledge, 1880.
Myddleton Pomfret. London: Routledge, 1881.
Hilary St. Ives. London: Routledge, 1881.
The South-Sea Bubble. London: Dicks [1871].
Tower Hill. London: Dicks [1871].
Talbot Harland. London: Routledge, 1879.
Boscobel. London: Routledge, 1879.
The Manchester Rebels of the Fatal '45, London: Routledge, 1880.

Merry England. London: Tinsley, 1874. 3 volumes.
The Goldsmith's Wife. London: Tinsley, 1875. 3 volumes.
Preston Fight. London: Routledge, 1879.
The Leaguer of Lathom. London: Routledge, 1880.
Chetwynd Calverley. London: Tinsley, 1876. 3 volumes.
The Fall of Somerset. London: Tinsley, 1877. 3 volumes.
Beatrice Tyldesley. London: Tinsley, 1878. 3 volumes.
Beau Nash. London: Routledge, 1880.
Stanley Brereton. London: Routledge, 1882.

SECONDARY SOURCES

Axon, W. E. A. *William Harrison Ainsworth: A Memoir.* London: Gibbings, 1902. Brief biographical sketch, expanded from his *Dictionary of National Biography* entry on Ainsworth.

Biles, Jack I. "William Harrison Ainsworth: His Artistry and Significance." Emory University, Ph.D. Dissertation, 1954. General appraisal.

Chandler, Frank W. *The Literature of Roguery.* 2 vols. Boston: Houghton, Mifflin, 1907. Contains an account of *Rookwood* and *Jack Sheppard* (II, 361–70).

Ellis, S. M. *William Harrison Ainsworth and His Friends.* 2 vols. London: John Lane, 1911. By far the most complete biographical account, based on letters and recollections.

Elwin, Malcolm. *Victorian Wallflowers.* London: Cape, 1934. The chapter on Ainsworth makes heavy, though not always accurate, use of Ellis.

Evans, John. "The Early Life of William Harrison Ainsworth." *Manchester Quarterly,* I (1882), 136–55. Concentrates on the Manchester years.

Faurot, Ruth M. "The Early Novels of William Harrison Ainsworth." University of North Carolina, Ph.D. Dissertation, 1953. Examines the fourteen novels written before 1852.

Friswell, J. Hain. *Modern Men of Letters.* London: Hodder & Stoughton, 1870. The essay on Ainsworth deplores the immoral effect of his tales of highwaymen.

Gribble, Francis. "Harrison Ainsworth." *Fortnightly Review,* LXXVII n.s. (March, 1905), 533–42. Ainsworth "the greatest of the commonplace and the most commonplace of the great": "he was, with half his nature, the sort of boy who improvises blood-curdling tales in the dormitory at the dead of night, and with the other half a Fellow of the Society of Antiquaries."

Hollingsworth, Keith. *The Newgate Novel.* Detroit: Wayne State, 1963. Places *Rookwood* and *Jack Sheppard* in the Newgate tradition.

Horne, R. H. *A New Spirit of the Age.* New York: Harper, 1872. Originally published in 1844, this contains a castigation of Ainsworth as a historical novelist. Example: *Old Saint Paul's* "is generally dull, except when it is revolting" (p. 315).

Joline, Adrian H. *At the Library Table.* Boston: Badger, 1910. Chapter V contains a generally favorable account of Ainsworth's work and a sketch of his life and character based on some of the same materials used by Ellis.

Locke, Harold. *A Bibliographical Catalogue of the Published Novels and Ballads of William Harrison Ainsworth.* London: Mathews, 1925. Primarily directed to the collector, but useful to others interested in tracing publishing history.

Paton, James, III. "The Historical Novels of William Harrison Ainsworth." Western Reserve University, Ph.D. Dissertation, 1954. Ainsworth as a historical novelist.

Ricks, Beatrice. "Characteristics of the Gothic Historical Novel in the Works of William Harrison Ainsworth." University of Oklahoma, Ph.D. Dissertation, 1954. Chiefly on Gothic elements, but also contains chapters on humor and spectacle.

Index